Understanding the Vocabulary of the Nuclear Arms Race

By Paul Fleisher

DILLON PRESS, INC.
Minneapolis, Minnesota 55415

Dedication
This book is dedicated to the members of Richmond STOP, the Student/
Teacher Organization to Prevent Nuclear War. May you live your lives
in peace.

Acknowledgments
Thanks to my brother Daniel Fleisher and to my friend and colleague Donna
Fout for reading my manuscript and making many valuable suggestions.

The photographs are reproduced through the courtesy of Argonne National
Laboratory; Kenneth T. Bainbridge; *Bulletin of the Atomic Scientists*; Council
for a Livable World; Lawrence Livermore National Laboratory; Los Alamos
National Laboratory; United Nations; and the U.S. Air Force.

Library of Congress Cataloging-in-Publication Data

Fleisher, Paul.
   Understanding the vocabulary of the nuclear arms race.

   (Peacemakers)
   Bibliography: p.
   Includes index.
   Summary: Presents definitions of terms most commonly
encountered in discussions of the nuclear arms race.
   1. Nuclear warfare—Dictionaries—Juvenile literature.
[1. Nuclear warfare—Dictionaries] I. Title.
II. Series.
U263.F57   1988   355'.0217'0321   87-15430
ISBN 0-87518-352-2

Dillon Press, Inc., 242 Portland Avenue South
Minneapolis, Minnesota 55415

Printed in the United States of America

Contents

Introduction

A nuclear explosion is enormously destructive. The United States dropped two atomic bombs on Japan at the end of World War II. Each one destroyed an entire city—and those bombs were small compared to the bombs that the United States, the Soviet Union, and several other countries have today.

Fortunately, since the end of World War II, no nuclear weapons have been used in warfare. Still, their threat is with us every day of our lives.

Today, there are more than 50,000 nuclear weapons in the world. Together these weapons contain at least a million times the power of the first atomic bomb. Both the United States and the Soviet Union possess enough nuclear warheads to destroy the entire world several times over. And yet, the race to build new, more destructive, and more accurate weapons continues.

Controlling nuclear weapons may be the most difficult and important problem facing our country and the world. No one wants a nuclear war. Everyone agrees that nuclear arms must be controlled. But there is a great deal of disagreement about *how* the weapons should be controlled, and *how* the world could be made less dangerous.

We hear about nuclear weapons on the evening news. We read about them in the newspaper. All citizens, young and old, need to know what is being done to keep their nations safe. Governments work best when citizens tell their leaders how they want them to solve tough problems. That's true with the arms race, too. It's our responsibility to let our leaders know what we want them to do about nuclear weapons.

But before we can do that, we have to know what we're talking about. News reports about nuclear weapons and treaty talks can be hard to understand. Experts who talk about nuclear weapons often use special language unfamiliar to most of us. This book will help you understand the arms race by explaining the words and ideas that reporters, government officials, and other experts use to discuss it.

Most of the information in this book applies to the nuclear forces and nuclear strategy of the United States. The Soviet Union has similar weapons and strategies, and several other nations, including Great Britain, France, and China, also have nuclear weapons. Although the United States and the Soviet Union are the two main powers in the nuclear arms race, the weapons of these other countries must be taken into account.

You can use this book as a reference, looking up particular words as you need them. You may also decide to read it all the way through, as an introduction to the nuclear arms race. Either way, it should teach you a lot about one of the greatest problems the human race has ever faced.

Able Nuclear Test

The Able test was the first U.S. test of a NUCLEAR BOMB* in peacetime. Able was exploded above Bikini Island in the Pacific Ocean, on July 1, 1946. The name *Able* comes from the military alphabet code for the letter *A*.

ABM (see ANTIBALLISTIC MISSILE)

ABM Treaty

Antiballistic Missile Treaty. This TREATY between the United States and the Soviet Union limits the ANTIBALLISTIC MISSILE SYSTEMS each country can have. ABM systems are weapons designed to shoot down an enemy's BALLISTIC MISSILES.

The ABM Treaty was negotiated during the SALT I talks and signed in 1972. In the treaty, each country agreed to build only two ABM sites. In 1974, both countries agreed to build only one site each.

The United States placed its ABM site in North Dakota, to protect MISSILE SILOS there. The U.S. ABM base was closed in the 1970s. The Soviets built their one site near Moscow, to protect their nation's capital. Part of that system is still in operation.

As of 1987, both countries are planning antimissile defenses that may break the ABM Treaty. The United States is developing the

7

Terms in capital letters appear as separate entries in this book.

STRATEGIC DEFENSE INITIATIVE — also known as "Star Wars" — and the Soviets are building a new advance RADAR system. The U.S. government claims this radar is part of a new ballistic missile defense.

A-Bomb (see ATOMIC BOMB)

Absolute Weapon (see DOOMSDAY MACHINE)

Absorbed Dose

An absorbed dose refers to the amount of RADIATION that a person takes into his or her body when exposed to radioactive substances. An absorbed dose of radiation is measured in RADS.

Accidental Nuclear War

A nuclear war could start by accident in many different ways. For example, a military commander might use NUCLEAR WEAPONS in battle without permission. RADAR systems that warn against nuclear attack could give a false alarm that would not be corrected in time. A nuclear weapon could simply be fired by mistake.

If one of these things were to happen, a country with nuclear weapons might think it was being attacked on purpose. It might launch a large nuclear strike before the accident was discovered.

The United States and the Soviet Union have agreed to tell each other immediately if a nuclear weapon is launched or exploded by accident (see UNITED STATES-SOVIET UNION NUCLEAR ACCIDENTS AGREEMENT). The HOTLINE between Washington, D.C., and Moscow would be used to communicate this information as quickly as possible.

Accuracy

Accuracy is how close a MISSILE or other weapon comes to hitting its target. The accuracy of nuclear missiles is usually measured by an average called CIRCULAR ERROR PROBABLE (CEP). A CEP of one-fourth mile (two-fifths kilometer) means that if 100 MISSILES were fired at a target, 50 of them would land within one-fourth mile of it.

Agreement

An agreement is an official paper signed by two or more countries. In an agreement, each country promises to do certain things or follow certain rules.

An agreement is less formal than a TREATY. Unlike a treaty, an agreement made by the United States does not have to be ratified (approved) by the U.S. Senate.

Airborne Early Warning and Control System (AWACS)

An Airborne Early Warning and Control System (AWACS) is a large airplane that carries RADAR and communications equipment. AWACS planes are used to watch for enemy attacks. They may also serve as an Air Force command post. Officers on the plane can use its electronic equipment to guide bombers and fighter planes to their targets.

Airburst

An airburst refers to the explosion of a NU-CLEAR WEAPON in the air above a target. An airburst may explode several hundred to several thousand feet above the ground. Exploding a WARHEAD in this way widens its destructive power because less of its force is absorbed by the earth. Instead, the BLAST, heat, and RADIATION are spread over a much larger area. The U.S. NUCLEAR BOMBS dropped on the Japanese cities of HIROSHIMA and NAGA-SAKI in 1945 were both airbursts.

The atomic bomb dropped over the Japanese city of Hiroshima in 1945 exploded in an airburst that destroyed the city. This picture was taken less than a mile from ground zero.

Air-Launched Ballistic Missile (ALBM)

An air-launched ballistic missile (ALBM) is a nuclear armed MISSILE carried on an airplane. The airplane acts as a mobile launch pad for the missile. Carrying the missile in an airplane helps keep it safe from enemy attack. To launch, the missile's engines would fire after it was dropped from the plane.

As of 1987, the United States has no long-range ALBMs. However, the Air Force may decide to place BALLISTIC MISSILES in airplanes in the future.

Air-to-Air Missile (AAM)

An air-to-air missile (AAM), is a guided MISSILE fired from one airplane to attack another. Most AAMs are armed with non-nuclear high explosives. However, an air-to-air missile could also be armed with a nuclear WARHEAD.

Air-to-Surface Missile (ASM)

An air-to-surface missile (ASM), is a guided MISSILE fired from an airplane to destroy a target on the earth's surface. Air-to-surface missiles can be used to attack ships or targets on land. ASMs may be armed with nuclear explosives or conventional (non-nuclear) explosives.

Alpha Radiation

Alpha radiation is a form of RADIOACTIVITY given off by radioactive elements such as PLUTONIUM and URANIUM. Alpha "rays" are actually tiny particles made of two PROTONS and two NEUTRONS. An alpha particle is exactly the same as the NUCLEUS of a helium ATOM. It has a positive electrical charge.

Alpha particles are the least powerful kind of RADIATION. They cannot travel more than six inches (fifteen centimeters) through the air. One or two sheets of paper, or the upper layers of a person's skin, will stop them.

However, inside the body alpha particles are the most damaging kinds of radiation. Elements that release alpha particles may be taken into the body by breathing or eating. Even tiny specks of plutonium will cause cancer if the plutonium dust is breathed into the lungs.

Large amounts of alpha radiation are produced in a nuclear explosion. The radioactive FALLOUT that follows the BLAST also produces alpha radiation.

Antarctic Treaty

The Antarctic Treaty is an AGREEMENT among certain nations to use Antarctica only for peaceful, scientific purposes. The TREATY was signed in 1959 by all countries that had claimed land in Antarctica. Both the United States and the Soviet Union are signers of the Antarctic Treaty.

Among other things, the treaty makes Antarctica a NUCLEAR-FREE ZONE. Under its terms, other weapons and military activities are also not allowed in the world's southernmost continent.

Antiballistic Missile (ABM)

An antiballistic missile (ABM) is a small, fast MISSILE designed to shoot down incoming enemy WARHEADS. Nuclear missile warheads are small — only about six feet (two meters) long — and they travel at more than 1,000 miles (1,610 kilometers) per hour as they approach their targets. To destroy such warheads, an antiballistic missile must be extremely quick and accurate. It also requires highly accurate RADAR and very fast computers to track the targets and aim the missiles.

Antiballistic missiles can destroy enemy warheads in two different ways. One method is to hit the enemy warhead directly with a non-explosive ABM warhead. Such a collision breaks the enemy warhead into pieces so that it cannot explode. The second method is to explode a nuclear-armed ABM near the enemy warhead, destroying or damaging it.

Both methods are difficult to use successfully. Because nuclear explosions create huge bursts of radio waves, a nuclear ABM explosion might "blind" the radar of other ABMs. Then the other ABMs wouldn't be able to find their targets.

Non-explosive ABMs wouldn't blind radar systems. Yet the small size and high speeds of the objects involved make it very difficult to achieve direct hits. Stopping an enemy warhead in this way is like shooting a speeding bullet with another bullet. However, in 1985 the United States successfully tested at least one such missile.

Antiballistic Missile System

An antiballistic missile system refers to a group of weapons designed to defend against ballistic nuclear MISSILES. Such a system may rely on ANTIBALLISTIC MISSILES as well as other antimissile weapons and RADAR tracking stations.

Neither the United States nor the Soviet Union has an effective ABM system, and it is unlikely that one will be built soon. However, the United States has begun research and testing for a new ABM system known as the

STRATEGIC DEFENSE INITIATIVE (SDI), or "Star Wars." SDI may include powerful LASERS, KINETIC ENERGY WEAPONS, and PARTICLE BEAM WEAPONS, as well as antiballistic missiles.

One problem with building an ABM system is that it has always been possible for the United States or the Soviet Union to defeat it. For example, an ABM system may be made useless if an enemy can build more missiles, use DECOY WARHEADS, or fire missiles that fly too low to be seen by radar.

Antisatellite Weapons (ASAT)

Antisatellite weapons (ASAT) are designed to destroy satellites orbiting the earth. They do this by moving near a satellite and then ramming it, exploding, or damaging it in some other way.

The Soviet Union has "hunter-killer" satellites which can move near another satellite and then explode. The United States has tested a small MISSILE fired from a jet fighter that can destroy satellites by crashing into them.

U.S. and Soviet satellites have important military uses. Some spy on opposing forces. Others communicate with military units around the world. Yet another group provides early warning of enemy attacks. If many of those satellites were destroyed, a country's military forces would be severely weakened.

Antisub-marine Rocket (ASROC)

An antisubmarine rocket (ASROC) is a rocket-propelled nuclear WARHEAD fired from a ship to destroy an enemy submarine — a type of NUCLEAR DEPTH CHARGE.

Upon firing the ASROC flies through the air to the location of a submarine. It then dives underwater and seeks out the submarine. When it is close enough, it explodes (see also SUBROC).

Antisub-marine Warfare (ASW)

Antisubmarine warfare (ASW) is an important part of modern military STRATEGY. Both the United States and Soviet Union have dozens of submarines that carry nuclear MISSILES. These submarines are very difficult to find and track. In time of war, each nation would try to destroy as many of the other's submarines as it could.

Many vessels and aircraft in the Soviet and U.S. navies are designed to search for and destroy enemy submarines. Antisubmarine warfare is carried out by surface ships, ATTACK SUBMARINES, helicopters, airplanes, and even electronic listening posts on the sea floor.

ANZUS Pact

The ANZUS pact refers to a TREATY, signed in 1951 by Australia (A), New Zealand (NZ), and the United States (US). In this treaty, the three countries promise to help defend each other in wartime. The agreement also allows U.S. planes and warships to use ports and bases in the other two countries.

In 1986 the government of New Zealand challenged at least part of the ANZUS treaty. It decided not to allow any nuclear-armed warships in its harbors. The U.S. government says that New Zealand's action breaks its treaty agreement. As a result, the United States no longer promises to keep New Zealand safe from attack.

Arms Control

Arms control means to reduce or put limits on the kinds and numbers of weapons that countries have. Usually it is accomplished through NEGOTIATIONS and TREATIES.

In the past, efforts to control the nuclear arms race have not been very successful. The SALT treaties limited the kinds and numbers of NUCLEAR WEAPONS that the United States and the Soviet Union possess. Treaties have also limited NUCLEAR TESTING and the spread of nuclear weapons. However, countries that have nuclear weapons are still building newer, more advanced ones, and some countries that do not possess nuclear weapons yet will probably have them soon.

Arms Control and Disarmament Agency (ACDA)

The Arms Control and Disarmament Agency (ACDA) was created by President John F. Kennedy in 1961. This U.S. government agency is responsible for advising the U.S. president about arms control matters. ACDA experts also participate in talks with other countries about arms control TREATIES.

Arms Control Through Defense

Arms control through defense is an idea used to support antimissile defenses such as President Reagan's STRATEGIC DEFENSE INITIATIVE ("Star Wars"). According to this idea, having an effective way to shoot down attacking BALLISTIC MISSILES would help the United States reach an agreement with the Soviet Union to reduce the numbers of long-range ballistic missiles. If each country had ways of shooting down these MISSILES, there would be less reason for each side to have so many of them.

Arms Race

An arms race is a competition between countries to build more weapons, and more powerful weapons, than those of the other side. Since 1945, the United States and the Soviet Union have been in a nuclear arms race.

Both the United States and the Soviet Union have built large stockpiles of NUCLEAR WEAPONS. Between them, the two countries now possess about 50,000 nuclear WARHEADS. The total explosive power of these weapons is about 7,000 times the explosive power of all the weapons used in World War II.

Both nations have also raced to develop more advanced weapons. Modern nuclear weapons are much faster, much smaller, much more accurate, and much harder to defend against than the earliest NUCLEAR BOMBS.

The United States and the Soviet Union are still competing in the race to build nuclear weapons. Here is a list of the major weapons developed by the two superpowers since 1945.

U.S.A.	Weapon	U.S.S.R.
1945	Fission (atomic) bomb	1949
1948	Intercontinental bomber	1955
1952	Thermonuclear bomb	1953
1958	Intercontinental ballistic missile (ICBM)	1957
1958	Artificial satellite	1957
1960	Submarine-launched ballistic missile	1968
1966	Multiple warhead (MRV)	1968
1972	Antiballistic missile (ABM)	1968
1970	Multiple independently targetable warhead (MIRV)	1975
1982	Cruise missile	1984
1986	Antisatellite missile	??
??	Stealth bomber	??
??	Particle beam and laser weapons	??

Arrival Time

Arrival time refers to the amount of time it takes for a NUCLEAR WEAPON to reach its target once it has been launched. Long-range bombers have arrival times of several hours. U.S. and Soviet long-range land-based missiles, such as the MINUTEMAN MISSILE and MX, have arrival times of about half an hour. The Trident and other SUBMARINE-LAUNCHED BALLISTIC MISSILES reach their targets about fifteen minutes after launching. And INTERMEDIATE-RANGE BALLISTIC MISSILES, such as the PERSHING II, have arrival times of about six minutes. As arrival times become shorter, countries have less time to allow for mistakes or false alarms from early warning systems.

ASROC (see ANTISUBMARINE ROCKET)

Atom

An atom is the basic building block of all known materials. It is the smallest particle of any element that can exist either alone or in combination. Atoms are so small they cannot be seen, even by the most powerful microscope.

Atoms are made up of a NUCLEUS, surrounded by a cloud of negatively charged particles called ELECTRONS. The nucleus itself is made up of neutral particles called NEUTRONS and positively-charged particles called PROTONS.

It takes a large amount of force to hold the particles of an atomic nucleus together. This force is called "binding energy." The power of a nuclear explosion comes from releasing some of the energy stored in the nucleus of atoms.

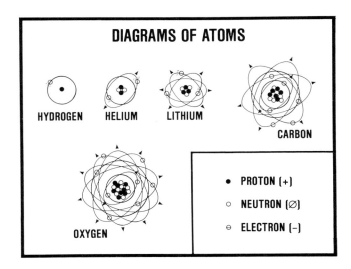

DIAGRAMS OF ATOMS

HYDROGEN   HELIUM   LITHIUM

CARBON

OXYGEN

- PROTON (+)
○ NEUTRON (∅)
⊖ ELECTRON (−)

Atomic Age

The atomic age refers to the modern era of history that began in 1945, with the explosion of the first NUCLEAR WEAPON. This period is called the atomic age because nuclear weapons have been such an important influence on world events since the end of World War II.

Atomic Bomb

Atomic bomb refers to a NUCLEAR BOMB fueled with URANIUM or PLUTONIUM. Another name for this weapon is a "fission bomb." An atomic bomb gets its power from the splitting (FISSION) of the uranium or plutonium ATOMS. Most NUCLEAR WEAPONS in the 1980s are THERMONUCLEAR (hydrogen) WEAPONS rather than atomic bombs.

The phrase "atomic bomb" was widely used in the early years of the ATOMIC AGE. Today the term "nuclear weapon" is more often used.

Atomic Energy (see NUCLEAR ENERGY)

Attack Submarine

An attack submarine is an underwater ship designed to attack other ships, including other submarines. Modern attack submarines are powered by NUCLEAR REACTORS. They can cruise underwater for weeks or months without coming to the surface.

Attack submarines are armed with torpedos to attack other ships. Some torpedos may be armed with nuclear WARHEADS. In addition, attack submarines carry SUBROCS, nuclear-armed antisubmarine missiles. A number of U.S. attack submarines also carry sea-launched CRUISE MISSILES. These MISSILES can destroy targets more than 1,000 miles (1,610 kilometers) away. To avoid being located by an enemy, they can be launched while the submarine is submerged.

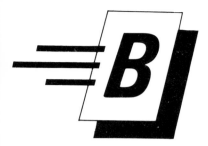

B-1B

The B-1B is the newest U.S. STRATEGIC (long-range) BOMBER. It has a range of more than 6,000 miles (9,660 kilometers) and can fly at supersonic speeds. The B-1B can carry bombs, CRUISE MISSILES, or SHORT-RANGE ATTACK MISSILES. This bomber is often called simply the B-1.

B-52

The B-52 is currently the main U.S. STRATEGIC (long-range) BOMBER. The first B-52s were built in 1952. Since then they have been mod-

A B-52 "Strato-fortress" flies high over snow-covered mountains.

ernized several times. Although the newest B-52s now are more than twenty years old, they have proved to be very reliable aircraft.

The B-52 has a range of 10,000 miles (16,100 kilometers). It can carry bombs, or as many as twenty SHORT-RANGE ATTACK MISSILES armed with nuclear WARHEADS. Many B-52s also carry air-launched CRUISE MISSILES.

Backfire, Badger, Bear, Blackjack, Blinder

The U.S. military uses words beginning with the letter *B* to name Soviet bombers. The names themselves have no meaning. For example, the "Backfire" bomber cannot fire bombs backward.

Background Radiation

Background radiation is the amount of RADIATION to which people are ordinarily exposed in their daily lives. The average person is exposed to about 170 MILLIREMS of background radiation each year. (A dentist's X ray gives off about 10 millirems.)

Background radiation comes from several sources. These include natural radioactive substances in the environment, and cosmic rays from outer space. Some background radiation also comes from the FALLOUT left from above-ground NUCLEAR TESTS in the 1940s, 1950s, and early 1960s.

Balance of Power

When two competing countries have military forces that are about equal, they are said to have a "balance of power." Each side knows that if it attacks first, the other side has enough strength to fight back successfully. Most people believe that such a balance of forces makes it less likely that either side will attack the other.

If the forces of two opposing countries are not balanced, the stronger country may try to take advantage of the weaker one. It might attack the weaker country directly, or it might try to take economic, military, or political advantage in other parts of the world. Either way, it knows the other country is not strong enough to pose a military threat.

Balance of Terror

Both the United States and the Soviet Union have enough NUCLEAR WEAPONS to destroy one another many times over. Because the fear of total destruction may help prevent each side from attacking the other, this balance of power is sometimes called a "balance of terror."

Ballistic Missile

A ballistic missile is a pilotless rocket that follows an arching (ballistic) path. It is launched toward its target with a burst of power from its engines. After the engines use up their fuel, the MISSILE coasts the rest of the way to its target in a high arc. Most nuclear ballistic missiles go high enough to leave the earth's atmosphere during much of their flight. Such a missile must be aimed correctly during the powered part of its flight, or it will miss its target.

Both the United States and the Soviet Union have several different kinds of ballistic missiles armed with nuclear WARHEADS. U.S. land-based ballistic missiles include the MINUTEMAN MISSILE, MX, LANCE, and PERSHING I AND II. The submarine-launched POSEIDON and TRIDENT are also ballistic missiles.

Soviet ballistic missiles are known by the letters *SS* followed by a number such as the SS-19 (see SS MISSILE). Soviet SUBMARINE-LAUNCHED BALLISTIC MISSILES are known by the letters *SS-N* followed by a number such as the SS-N-6 (see SS-N MISSILE). In addition to the U.S. and Soviet weapons, the French, British, and Chinese have smaller numbers of nuclear ballistic missiles.

Ballistic Missile Submarine (SSB)

A ballistic missile submarine (SSB), is an underwater ship that carries SUBMARINE-LAUNCHED BALLISTIC MISSILES. Powered by NUCLEAR REACTORS, these submarines can stay underwater for months at a time. Because they are so hard locate in the vast ocean, SSBs are very difficult to defend against.

Both the Soviet Union and the United States have dozens of ballistic missile submarines. The British, French, and Chinese also have smaller numbers of SSBs.

U.S. SSBs are known as POSEIDON and TRIDENT submarines, because they carry MISSILES called by these same names. The newest U.S. SSBs, Trident submarines, are also called "Ohio-class" submarines. Each Trident carries twenty-four missiles, and each missile carries ten nuclear WARHEADS.

Bargaining Chip

A bargaining chip is a weapon that a country is willing to give up, if another country agrees to give up a weapon of its own in return. Such trading usually takes place during ARMS CONTROL talks. For example, a diplomat might make this offer: "We'll stop building our new antisatellite MISSILE, if you agree not to build any more of your new long-range bombers."

A bargaining chip must be a real, working weapon. If it isn't, the other country won't be interested in trading to get rid of it. Building a new weapon however, requires a big investment in time and money. Once a new, effective weapon is built, military planners may not want to bargain it away.

Battlefield Nuclear Weapons (see TACTICAL NUCLEAR WEAPONS)

Beam Weapon (see PARTICLE BEAM WEAPON and LASER)

Beta Radiation

Beta radiation is a form of RADIOACTIVITY produced by naturally radioactive elements, nuclear explosions, and the FALLOUT that follows a nuclear BLAST. Beta particles are more powerful than ALPHA RADIATION. They can travel about one-half inch (more than one centimeter) into the human body. Exposure to large amounts of beta radiation causes burns.

Bethe, Hans (1906-   )

Hans Bethe is a scientist who helped build the first ATOMIC BOMB during the secret World War II program known as the MANHATTAN PROJECT. Born in Germany, he moved to the United States in 1934, after Hitler came to power. Bethe discovered that the sun and other stars produce energy through thermonuclear reactions. He was awarded a Nobel Prize in 1967 for that discovery.

After World War II, Bethe helped found the *Bulletin of Atomic Scientists*, a magazine which warns about the dangers of nuclear war. In recent years, Bethe has spoken out against the STRATEGIC DEFENSE INITIATIVE ("Star Wars").

Bikini Atoll

Bikini Atoll is a small island in the South Pacific Ocean where the United States held many of its NUCLEAR TESTS in the 1940s and 1950s. The first peacetime nuclear test, called the Able test, was held there in 1946.

A high-flying airplane took this picture of the Able nuclear test on Bikini Atoll in the South Pacific Ocean.

Bilateral

Bilateral means having two sides. It is a term usually used to describe ARMS CONTROL agreements between two countries. A bilateral agreement is one in which both sides agree to do something. When a country takes an action on its own, it acts in a UNILATERAL way.

The Threshold Test Ban Treaty of 1974 is an example of a BILATERAL AGREEMENT. In this TREATY the United States and the Soviet Union agreed not to test any NUCLEAR WEAPONS more powerful than 150 KILOTONS — an explosion equal to 150,000 tons of TNT.

Black Book

The "black book" refers to a list of choices that the U.S. president has in time of nuclear war. The choices come from a military plan called the SINGLE INTEGRATED OPERATING PLAN (SIOP). The black book is available to the president at all times, along with the codes needed to order a nuclear attack. The codes and plan are carried in a briefcase which is called the "FOOTBALL."

Blast

Blast is one of many deadly effects of a nuclear explosion. An exploding nuclear WARHEAD creates a shock wave of extremely high pressure that kills people and destroys buildings in its path. The blast from a ONE-MEGATON NUCLEAR WEAPON would flatten almost every building within five miles (eight kilometers) of the explosion. The strength of the blast wave is measured as "OVERPRESSURE."

The pressure wave from a nuclear explosion also causes winds as high as 600 miles

(966 kilometers) per hour. These powerful winds can cause severe injuries as far as fifteen miles (twenty-four kilometers) from GROUND ZERO. The pressure from the wind is sometimes called "DYNAMIC PRESSURE."

Blast Shelter

A blast shelter is a building designed to withstand the BLAST of a nuclear explosion. Blast shelters are built of thick concrete and steel, and they are buried below the ground for extra protection. Still, they cannot survive a direct hit from a NUCLEAR WEAPON.

BMEWS

Ballistic Missile Early Warning System. BMEWS is a series of powerful RADAR stations in Alaska, Greenland, and Great Britain that watch for MISSILE launches in the Soviet Union. They are designed to provide the United States with an early warning of a Soviet nuclear attack.

Booster

A booster is the first stage of a BALLISTIC MISSILE or rocket. The booster has a powerful rocket engine which starts the MISSILE on its flight. After the booster uses all its fuel, it drops away, and the rest of the missile continues its flight. Modern missile boosters burn SOLID FUEL.

Boost Phase

The boost phase is the first part of the flight of a BALLISTIC MISSILE. During this phase, the

MISSILE'S engines fire continuously, lifting the missile high above the earth.

Bravo Nuclear Test

The Bravo nuclear test took place on BIKINI ATOLL in the South Pacific Ocean on February 28, 1954. It was the first test of the TELLER-ULAM CONFIGURATION. This design made it possible to build THERMONUCLEAR (hydrogen) WEAPONS that were small enough to fit into a bomb.

The Bravo test spread radioactive FALLOUT over a Japanese fishing boat called the *Lucky Dragon*. The twenty-three crew members developed serious RADIATION SICKNESS, and one of them died. The fallout also polluted the island of RONGELAP, more than 100 miles (161 kilometers) from the test. The U.S. government had to move all the people of Rongelap to another island.

Breeder Reactor

A breeder reactor is a nuclear power reactor that produces (breeds) more nuclear fuel than it uses. URANIUM 238 is loaded into the reactor, which changes it into PLUTONIUM 239. In this form it can be used to generate electricity in other NUCLEAR REACTORS, or to arm nuclear WARHEADS.

Broken Arrow

Broken arrow is the U.S. military term for an accident involving a nuclear WARHEAD. There have been hundreds of broken arrows since the beginning of the ATOMIC AGE.

U.S. nuclear warheads are protected with

safeguards to prevent accidental explosions. So far, no broken arrow has caused a nuclear explosion, but at least seventy-five people have been killed in these accidents. Some of the broken arrows have also caused radioactive contamination (pollution).

For example, when a B-52 crashed in North Carolina in 1961, it dropped two NUCLEAR BOMBS. One of the bombs broke apart when it hit the ground. The soil was contaminated, and part of the bomb was never found. Similar airplane accidents occurred in Spain in 1966 and in Greenland in 1968.

In 1980 a TITAN II MISSILE exploded in its silo in Arkansas. The explosion threw the missile's nuclear warhead more than 200 yards (182 meters) away. Nuclear warheads have also been lost in submarine accidents.

Build-Down

Build-down refers to a U.S. ARMS CONTROL proposal made in the early 1980s. The United States offered to take two older nuclear MISSILES out of service for each new one that was built. This would have allowed the Soviet and U.S. armed forces to lower the number of NUCLEAR WEAPONS, while still making their weapons more modern. Soviet officials rejected the build-down idea because they thought it would give the United States a nuclear advantage.

Bus (Post-Boost Vehicle)

Most long-range BALLISTIC MISSILES carry several nuclear WARHEADS, called MIRVs. The bus, or post-boost vehicle, is the part of a nuclear ballistic missile that carries and releases multiple warheads and DECOY warheads.

Button, The

"The button" is the nickname for the system that would launch a U.S. or Soviet nuclear attack. "Pushing the button" means launching such an attack.

The U.S. president does not have an actual button that must be pressed in order to launch nuclear MISSILES. Instead, there is a set of coded instructions which has to be sent out through U.S. military communications channels. A set of these codes is kept near the president at all times. If the president is unable to give the order to launch an attack, certain other military commanders are also permitted to do so.

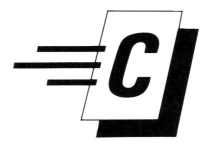

Chain Reaction

A chain reaction is a rapid series of connected events. In a chain reaction, each event causes the next event to happen.

In a nuclear chain reaction, the NUCLEUS (center) of a URANIUM or PLUTONIUM ATOM is struck by a NEUTRON (a tiny atomic particle). The nucleus then splits apart, releasing energy and more neutrons. If there is enough plutonium or uranium (see CRITICAL MASS), these other neutrons will strike other NUCLEI, causing them to release more energy and more neutrons. Those neutrons go on to strike still other nuclei.

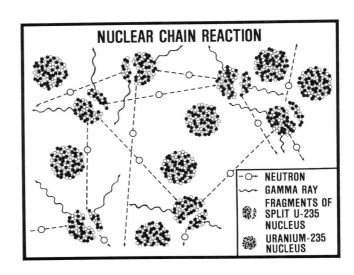

NUCLEAR CHAIN REACTION

- ○ NEUTRON
∿ GAMMA RAY
FRAGMENTS OF SPLIT U-235 NUCLEUS
URANIUM-235 NUCLEUS

Such a nuclear chain reaction happens in an instant. Within millionths of a second it can release the energy of a nuclear explosion. Nuclear chain reactions can also be controlled in a NUCLEAR REACTOR, producing a much slower, steady supply of energy.

Chernobyl

Chernobyl is the site of several Soviet nuclear power plants. It is located in the Ukraine, near the city of Kiev. In April 1986, a fire at one of these reactors released huge amounts of RADIATION into the environment.

This fire was the worst nuclear accident yet seen on the earth. More than thirty people died from radiation poisoning, and thousands more had severe RADIATION SICKNESS. A wide area was polluted with RADIOACTIVITY. At least 100,000 people had to be evacuated from the area. FALLOUT from the accident spread across much of Europe, depositing radiation on many crops.

Cheyenne Mountain

Cheyenne Mountain, in Colorado, is the headquarters of the American Air Defense Command (NORAD). The NORAD command center is buried deep inside the mountain. It is protected from attacks of every kind except direct hits from NUCLEAR WEAPONS.

Cheyenne Mountain is a communications and command center. It gathers information from U.S. early warning RADAR systems and early warning satellites. It also sends orders to the military commanders of U.S. air defenses and strategic missiles and bombers.

Circular Error Probable (CEP)

Circular error probable (CEP) is a measurement of the ACCURACY of a MISSILE. CEP is the radius of a circle into which half of a missile's WARHEADS will fall. For example, suppose a missile has a CEP of 500 yards (457 meters). Half the warheads carried by that type of missile will land within 500 yards of their target.

Modern missiles have become more and more accurate. Early missiles had CEPs measured in miles. But the latest U.S. missile, the MX, has a CEP of about the length of a football field.

Less accurate missiles can threaten "SOFT TARGETS" such as cities. But "HARD TARGETS" are protected by concrete and steel shelters. Missiles aimed at hard targets, such as underground MISSILE SILOS, must be extremely accurate to destroy those targets.

Many U.S. and Soviet missiles are now aimed at hard targets. This STRATEGY, called COUNTERFORCE targeting, depends on having accurate missiles with very small CEPs.

Civil Defense

Civil defense is a plan to protect the population of a country against nuclear attack and other disasters. A civil defense plan attempts to help as many people as possible survive an attack.

Plans for civil defense may include early warning of an attack and the evacuation of people from target areas such as large cities. Building FALLOUT shelters and storing supplies of food and medicine are other civil defense measures.

The Federal Emergency Management Administration (FEMA) is the U.S. government agency in charge of civil defense. In recent years the U.S. government has spent little money on civil defense. The Soviet government has a larger civil defense program for its people.

Cold Launch

A cold launch is a method of launching a MISSILE from an underground silo or a missile tube on a submarine. In a cold launch, the missile is pushed out of its silo or tube with a blast of air pressure. Then, after the missile is already moving upward, its engines fire, and it takes off.

A cold launch makes it possible to reuse a silo or launch tube for launching other missiles. Cold launching also allows a missile to carry a slightly heavier PAYLOAD.

Cold War

The rivalry between the United States and the Soviet Union since the end of World War II is known as the "cold war." It is called a cold war because the competition has not "heated" up into an actual military battle.

The cold war takes the form of threats, shows of military force, economic competition, and political disagreements. Since 1945, tension between the United States and the Soviet Union has been much greater at some times than others. During the CUBAN MISSILE CRISIS of 1962, the two countries came close to starting a nuclear war. At other times, both sides have been more willing to discuss their differences and try to reach agreements.

Collateral Damage

Collateral damage refers to the people and property that would be destroyed by a nuclear strike against MISSILE bases and other military targets. The "collateral damage" from such an attack could include many millions of civilian deaths, and millions of injuries.

Command, Control, Communications, and Intelligence (C₃I)

Command, Control, Communications, and Intelligence (C_3I) is the system that a country uses to direct its military forces during a war. The U.S. C_3I system is extremely complex. It includes a communications network and protected command posts in different locations around the country. The C_3I system also has mobile command posts in airplanes (see NATIONAL EMERGENCY AIRBORNE COMMAND POST).

The command posts are in contact with one another through many different radio channels and telephone connections. They also receive information, called intelligence, from U.S. military commanders, RADAR stations, and spy satellites.

In wartime, high-ranking military and civilian leaders receive huge amounts of information. This information must be studied quickly, using computers. The leaders must then communicate their orders to thousands of troops around the world. As a result, the command posts that control U.S. forces must also gather intelligence and serve as communications centers.

Military planners have attempted to design their C_3I networks so that they can do their work no matter what happens. However, many experts wonder whether such a system can continue to work effectively during a nuclear attack.

Comprehensive Test Ban Treaty (CTB)

A comprehensive test ban treaty (CTB) is a TREATY that would outlaw all test explosions of NUCLEAR WEAPONS. Such a treaty does not exist. However, it has been discussed since the early 1960s. Since 1945, almost 1,700 nuclear weapons have been tested by the United States, the Soviet Union, and the other nuclear nations.

Both houses of the U.S. Congress have voted in favor of a comprehensive test ban. Those who favor a CTB say that it would help slow the arms race by preventing the U.S. and Soviet armed forces from developing new, more dangerous weapons.

Those who oppose such a treaty think it would weaken U.S. ability to develop new weapons that would keep the country strong. They also doubt the Soviets would keep their word about following the treaty.

If a comprehensive test ban is ever signed, it will have to be verifiable. That means the countries signing the treaty would have to agree on ways to make sure that no one breaks the treaty and secretly tests new weapons. A CTB might be verified by information from satellites, seismic stations that measure earth shocks, radiation detectors, and human inspectors (see VERIFICATION).

Contamination

Contamination means pollution. Air, water, food, clothing, soil, and even the human body can be contaminated by radioactive substances.

There are many possible sources of radioactive contamination. It can be caused by FALLOUT from nuclear explosions. It can also come from leaks of RADIOACTIVE WASTE, or from accidents at nuclear power plants or nuclear weapons factories. Other than the bombings of Hiroshima and Nagasaki in 1945, the world's worst case of radioactive contamination occurred in 1986 at the Soviet nuclear power plant at CHERNOBYL.

Controlled Response

Controlled response is a U.S. STRATEGY for using limited numbers of NUCLEAR WEAPONS to respond to a limited attack from the Soviet Union or elsewhere. In a controlled response, the United States would use only a few nuclear weapons instead of using a full-scale nuclear attack.

Conventional Weapons

Conventional weapons are non-nuclear weapons of almost any kind. Guns, grenades, tanks, helicopters, and high-explosive bombs are all examples of conventional weapons. Chemical and biological weapons, though, are usually not considered conventional weapons.

Cooperative Measures

Cooperative measures are methods of verifying (checking) ARMS CONTROL TREATIES. To be effective, these methods require the cooperation of the countries that have signed the treaty. Allowing each other's scientists to inspect weapons factories or test sites is one example of a cooperative measure.

The other way to verify treaties is through NATIONAL TECHNICAL MEANS. These methods do not require the cooperation of the other country or countries.

Counterforce

Counterforce is a military STRATEGY that aims a country's weapons against its opponent's military forces, instead of non-military targets. In the nuclear arms race, counterforce means a country's MISSILES are aimed at the MISSILE SILOS of its opponent. Since missile silos are heavily protected by concrete and steel (see HARD TARGET), counterforce weapons must be extremely accurate. Both the United States and the Soviet Union have many of their missiles aimed at opposing missile forces.

The idea behind this strategy is that a counterforce attack might destroy enemy missiles before they can do any damage. Such an attack also poses less of a threat to civilians. And yet, a counterforce attack on the United States or the Soviet Union would still kill many millions of ordinary citizens.

Counterforce weapons aimed at a country's missiles may actually encourage that country to launch an attack. If a country's missiles are threatened during a crisis, it may be tempted to launch them rather than risk having them destroyed. (see USE IT OR LOSE IT).

Countervalue

Countervalue is a military STRATEGY in which one country's weapons are aimed at the population and resources of another country (its "values"). In countervalue strategy, weapons are aimed at cities, factories, and transportation centers. Both the United States and the Soviet Union have enough WARHEADS to use both COUNTERFORCE and countervalue strategies.

Credibility

Credibility means the ability to be believed, and it is sometimes used to describe a country's plans to use its military forces in response to an attack. The United States and the Soviet Union use their NUCLEAR WEAPONS as a threat to keep the other nations from attacking first. But a threat only works if the other side believes it. Each side must believe that the other can and will fight back if attacked. A country that will use its military strength if attacked is said to have credibility.

Crisis Relocation

Crisis relocation refers to the U.S. government's plans for evacuating people from large cities in case of nuclear war or some other major disaster. It is an important part of the U.S. civil defense program.

Critical Mass

Critical mass is the amount of URANIUM or PLUTONIUM needed to set off a CHAIN REACTION and cause a nuclear explosion. It takes only a few pounds of uranium or plutonium to form a critical mass.

The amount of fuel needed to form a critical mass also depends on its density, or how tightly packed it is. The denser the nuclear fuel, the less of it is needed to reach a critical mass.

A nuclear WARHEAD contains a small sphere (ball) of plutonium or uranium. This sphere is not dense enough to be "critical." The fuel is surrounded by non-nuclear high explosives. When the warhead explodes, the high explosives fire first. The explosive force squeezes the nuclear fuel together, making it denser. It becomes dense enough to form a critical mass and start the nuclear BLAST.

Cruise Missile

A cruise missile is not a MISSILE at all. It is a small, pilotless jet airplane, guided by a computer, that carries a single nuclear or non-nuclear WARHEAD. U.S. Tomahawk cruise missiles have a range of about 1,300 miles (2,100 kilometers).

Cruise missiles have advanced guidance systems that allow them to fly at extremely low altitude. Flying low keeps them from being detected by enemy RADAR.

Since cruise missiles are only about twenty feet (six meters) long and two feet (less than a meter) in diameter, they can be hidden quite easily. That makes them hard to verify (check) in any ARMS CONTROL agreement.

Cruise missiles can be launched from airplanes (air-launched cruise missiles or ALCMs). They can also be launched from MOBILE LAUNCHERS on land (ground-launched cruise missiles or GLCMs) or from submarines or surface ships (sea-launched cruise missiles or SLCMs).

The United States has cruise missiles at European military bases, and on submarines and battleships. Many of the STRATEGIC AIR COMMAND'S bombers carry air-launched cruise missiles. The Soviet Union has also developed its own cruise missiles.

AIR-LAUNCHED CRUISE MISSILE

Cuban Missile Crisis

In the early 1960s, the Soviet Union began building a medium-range nuclear MISSILE base on the island of Cuba. Cuba is just 90 miles (150 kilometers) from southern Florida, the closest point in the United States. U.S. officials discovered the missile base in October 1962, through photographs taken by spy planes.

When President Kennedy found out about the Soviet base, he told the Soviets that he would not allow them to have nuclear missiles in Cuba. The Soviets said the missile base was being built for Cuban defense. They pointed out that U.S. missiles were stationed near the Soviet border in Turkey.

At that time, twenty-four of the Soviet missiles were ready for launching. A Soviet ship carrying more missiles was also headed for Cuba. President Kennedy told the Soviet leader, Nikita Khrushchev, that U.S. warships would not allow the Soviet ship to land in Cuba.

For three days, no one knew if the Soviets would try to keep their missiles in Cuba. No one knew if the United States would use its NUCLEAR WEAPONS to force the Soviets to back down. The threat of nuclear war frightened many people in the United States and throughout the world. In the end, the Soviet ship turned back, and the Soviets removed their other missiles.

Some people reacted to the Cuban missile crisis by building bomb shelters. Others joined organizations that worked to control nuclear weapons. The crisis showed U.S. and Soviet leaders that they needed better communications to help control future problems. As a result, the two countries soon agreed to install the HOTLINE.

Curie

The curie is the unit used to measure the amount of RADIOACTIVITY in various materials. It is named in honor of the French scientist Marie Curie, who discovered the radioactive elements radium and polonium.

A curie is the amount of radioactivity in one gram of radium. Since radium is highly radioactive, that is a large amount of radioactivity. One curie is equal to 31 billion radioactive emissions per second.

One hour after the explosion of a one MEGA-TON nuclear WARHEAD, there would be about 300 billion curies of radioactivity left in the environment.

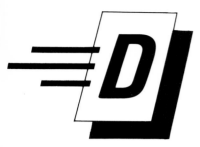

Decapitation

Decapitation is the strategy of killing a country's leaders at the beginning of a war. The military forces of that country would then be unsure about where their orders should come from, or they might not receive any orders at all. Because of this confusion, the country's defenses would be less effective.

Decoy

A decoy is a false unarmed WARHEAD designed to confuse enemy RADAR tracking. Modern nuclear MISSILES carry decoys in addition to their actual warheads. Radar can't tell the difference between decoys and real warheads until they re-enter the atmosphere. As they enter the atmosphere, the decoys burn up due to the friction of the air, while the real warheads continue on the paths to their targets.

DEFCON

Defense Readiness Condition (DEFCON) refers to the level of readiness of U.S. military forces. Defense conditions can range from DEFCON 5 to DEFCON 1. DEFCON 5 refers to the level of ordinary peacetime readiness. Under DEFCON 1, all U.S. forces would be prepared for war.

Delivery System

A delivery system is any vehicle or set of vehicles that transports nuclear WARHEADS to their targets. Delivery systems for U.S. NUCLEAR WEAPONS include long-, medium-, and short-range MISSILES, submarine-launched missiles, CRUISE MISSILES, bombers, artillery, torpedos, land and sea mines, and even hand-carried nuclear warheads.

Department of Defense (DOD)

The Department of Defense (DOD) is the part of the U.S. government responsible for all military activity. The secretary of defense directs the daily activities of the Department of Defense. The secretary and his assistants are civilians to make sure that the military stays under control of the elected, civilian government.

The Department of Defense is in charge of the Army, Navy, Air Force, and Marine Corps. Including military and civilian employees, it employs more than 2 million people. It also hires private companies to do much of its work. The Defense Department spends more than any other department of the U.S. government. In 1986, it had a budget of 314 billion dollars — about one-third of the entire federal budget.

Department of Energy (DOE)

The Department of Energy (DOE) is the part of the U.S. government that supervises all U.S. energy activities, including the production of oil, gas, coal, and electricity.

The Energy Department also builds and tests all U.S. NUCLEAR WEAPONS. This means that the money for making nuclear weapons is not part of the military budget. Instead, Congress places the funds for nuclear weapons in the budget of the Department of Energy. More than one-third of the DOE budget goes for nuclear weapons research and production. In 1986 the Department of Energy spent almost 8 billion dollars on nuclear weapons.

Deploy

Deploy means to put into place. When a country deploys a weapon, it puts the weapon in the location where it can be launched or fired.

Depressed Trajectory

A depressed trajectory is the path of a BALLISTIC MISSILE that flies lower to the earth than other similar MISSILES. Most ballistic missiles follow arching paths which take them high above the atmosphere. Missiles with depressed trajectories fly at a much lower altitude and reach their targets more quickly. These missiles are also harder to track by RADAR, which helps them avoid antimissile defenses such as the proposed STRATEGIC DEFENSE INITIATIVE ("Star Wars").

Destabilizing

Destabilizing describes any change in the arms race that makes war more likely. For example, imagine that the United States was about to DEPLOY a new weapon that could destroy Soviet MISSILES. The Soviets might be tempted to attack before the new weapon was put into place. Therefore, the new weapon would be destabilizing. Or suppose that the Soviet Union developed a new weapon that was much more effective than any U.S. weapons. Since such a weapon would give the Soviets a big advantage in the military balance, it would also be destabilizing.

Détente

Détente refers to improved relations between two or more countries that have acted as enemies toward each other. When two such nations reach an agreement or TREATY with one another, that is an example of détente. This term is often used to describe the lessening of tensions between the United States and the Soviet Union during the 1960s and 1970s.

Deterrence

Deterrence is the STRATEGY of using a threat to prevent another person or nation from attacking. People use deterrence all the time. "If you take my pencil, I'll hit you," is a simple example of deterrence. The threat of hitting is used to prevent the other person from taking the pencil. For deterrence to work, the person being threatened must believe the threat is real.

In nuclear strategy, deterrence means threatening to use NUCLEAR WEAPONS against another country if that country attacks your country. Both the United States and the Soviet Union have thousands of strategic nuclear weapons. They use these weapons to deter, or prevent, one another from attacking.

Deuterium

Deuterium is an ISOTOPE — a slightly different form — of the element hydrogen. Deuterium occurs naturally on earth, but it is quite rare. It was discovered in 1934 by Harold Urey, who won the Nobel Prize in chemistry for his discovery.

An ordinary hydrogen ATOM has a NUCLEUS with just one PROTON. Deuterium has a proton and a NEUTRON. Since the extra neutron makes the deuterium atom heavier, deuterium is often called "HEAVY HYDROGEN."

Deuterium is one of the fuels used in THERMONUCLEAR (hydrogen) WEAPONS and is also used in some kinds of NUCLEAR REACTORS. It is produced by separating "HEAVY WATER," which contains deuterium, from ordinary water.

Development

Development of a NUCLEAR WEAPON starts with research and design work, and continues with building sample versions of that weapon for testing. A weapon must go through development before it can be produced and DEPLOYED.

Device (see NUCLEAR DEVICE)

DEW Line

Distant Early Warning Line. The DEW line is a group of thirty-one RADAR stations in Alaska and northern Canada. These radar stations are equipped to warn against attacks from Soviet bombers or CRUISE MISSILES.

The Dew Line is located in the Arctic because the shortest distance between the Soviet Union and the United States is the POLAR ROUTE over the Arctic Ocean. In addition to the DEW line, the United States has several other early warning systems (see PAVE PAWS, PINE TREE LINE, SATELLITE EARLY WARNING SYSTEM, BMEWS).

Directed Energy Weapon (see LASER and PARTICLE BEAM WEAPON)

Disarmament

Disarmament refers to actions taken to eliminate some or all of a nation's military forces. Nuclear disarmament has long been one of the key issues of the nuclear era, and many individuals and groups have worked hard to achieve it. Efforts at ARMS CONTROL, however, have not been successful in achieving disarmament.

Doomsday Machine

The doomsday machine is an imaginary weapon that would be capable of destroying the earth. Such a weapon would be triggered automatically if any country attacked another with NUCLEAR WEAPONS. According to this idea, nations would not dare launch a nuclear attack if they knew it would destroy the world.

Although there is no actual doomsday machine, the world's nuclear arsenals work in very much the same way. The United States and the Soviet Union each have enough weapons to destroy most animal and plant life on earth. If both countries were to use their nuclear arsenals, it would probably have the same effect as a doomsday machine. This threat of destruction helps keep the two countries at peace.

Double Zero Option

The double zero option is an arms control plan suggested in 1987. The proposal would remove all U.S. and Soviet short-range and medium-range missiles around the world. In September 1987, the United States and the Soviet Union agreed in principle to such a plan (see ZERO OPTION).

Dynamic Pressure

Dynamic pressure is the pressure of moving air, or wind. A nuclear explosion creates extremely high dynamic pressures. Winds from a nuclear BLAST can reach up to 600 miles (966 kilometers) per hour. These winds can do tremendous damage.

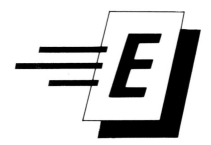

E=MC²

This is ALBERT EINSTEIN'S most famous equation. It shows that matter — anything that can have weight and takes up space — and energy are different forms of the same thing. That means matter can be changed into huge amounts of energy. A nuclear explosion has tremendous power because of this change.

In the equation, E stands for energy, M stands for mass — the amount of matter in a body — and C^2 stands for the speed of light multiplied times itself or squared. To figure out how much energy is "contained" in a piece of matter, you multiply the amount of matter times the speed of light squared.

Even tiny amounts of matter contain enormous amounts of energy. If the energy in one gram (.035 ounce) of matter could be released, the result would be equal to the energy of burning 3,000 tons of coal. Releasing all the energy from matter is not possible. In fact, a nuclear explosion changes only about one-thousandth of its nuclear fuel from matter into energy.

Einstein, Albert (1879-1955)

Albert Einstein, one of the greatest scientists who ever lived, made many brilliant contributions to physics. He was also respected around the world as a peace-loving human being. In 1921 Einstein won the Nobel Prize for physics. Twelve years later, he moved from Germany to the United States to avoid the Nazis. He spent the rest of his life working at the Institute for Advanced Studies in Princeton, New Jersey.

As one part of his theory of relativity, Einstein discovered that energy and matter are two different forms of the same thing (see E=MC²). This discovery is one of the ideas that led other scientists to realize that a NUCLEAR BOMB was possible. Einstein himself never attempted to build a NUCLEAR WEAPON.

In 1939, American scientists LEO SZILARD and Eugene Wigner thought German scientists were trying to build a nuclear bomb. When they told Albert Einstein about their concern, he wrote a letter to President Franklin Roosevelt to warn him of this pos-

In 1939 Albert Einstein *(left)* and Leo Szilard review Einstein's letter to President Franklin Roosevelt warning about German research that could produce a nuclear bomb.

sibility. The letter suggested that the United States put its scientists to work on a similar project.

Einstein was so famous that his letter got immediate results. Soon the United States began the MANHATTAN PROJECT, which eventually built the first nuclear bomb.

After World War II, Einstein often spoke about the dangers of nuclear weapons. He wanted to establish international control of nuclear weapons, and an international system of world laws.

Electromagnetic Pulse (EMP)

When a NUCLEAR WEAPON explodes, it produces an electrical "shock wave" known as an electromagnetic pulse (EMP). EMP is much like lightning in its effects. This tremendous burst of electrical energy can spread for hundreds or even thousands of miles. It travels at the speed of light (186,000 miles, or 300,000 kilometers, per second).

EMP doesn't affect living things directly, but it does affect electrical equipment such as telephones, RADAR, radio communications, and computers. When EMP passes through electrical equipment, it creates a powerful surge of current. This surge can blow fuses, burn out wires, and destroy delicate computer chips.

Just a few NUCLEAR BOMBS exploded high above the United States could destroy many of the country's computers, telephones, radios, and radars. Thus EMP could be used as a weapon to destroy a country's electronic defenses and its communications.

DEPARTMENT OF DEFENSE experts are studying EMP to find ways to protect electronic equipment from its effects. The Soviet Union is taking similar steps and may have developed better protection against EMP than the United States currently has.

Electron

The electron is one of the tiny particles that make up all ATOMS. Every atom is made of a NUCLEUS, surrounded by electrons. The positively charged nucleus of every atom (except hydrogen) contains both PROTONS and NEUTRONS. Electrons are negatively charged, and protons are positively charged. Neutrons have no electric charge.

EMP (see ELECTROMAGNETIC PULSE)

Enhanced Radiation Weapon (see NEUTRON BOMB)

Eniwetok Atoll

Eniwetok Atoll is a coral island located in the South Pacific Ocean in the Marshall Islands. In the 1950s it was used for U.S. NUCLEAR WEAPONS tests. Eniwetok's people were forced to move to another island before the testing began.

Enola Gay

Enola Gay was the name of the U.S. B-29 bomber that dropped the first ATOMIC BOMB on HIROSHIMA, Japan, on August 6, 1945.

Enriched Uranium

Enriched uranium is URANIUM that contains a high percentage of the ISOTOPE U-235.

When it is mined from the earth, uranium is made up of three different isotopes (varieties). More than 99 percent of it is U-238. U-238 is radioactive, but it cannot be used as fuel for nuclear explosions. U-235, the second isotope, can be used for fuel in NUCLEAR BOMBS. U-235 makes up less than 1 percent of natural uranium. Uranium also contains tiny amounts of a third isotope, U-234.

To be used in NUCLEAR REACTORS or NUCLEAR WEAPONS, uranium must be enriched. That means the amount of U-235 in it must be increased. Fuel for nuclear reactors must contain from 3 to 5 percent U-235. Uranium for nuclear WARHEADS has to be at least 85 to 90 percent U-235. This highly enriched fuel is known as WEAPONS-GRADE URANIUM.

Uranium can be enriched using several different methods. All enrichment methods are slow, difficult, and expensive.

One method of enrichment, gas diffusion, first changes uranium into a gas. It is then passed through a complex filtering system. Since U-235 is slightly lighter than U-238, it moves through filters slightly faster. As the filtering process is repeated many times, the U-235 becomes more and more concentrated.

A second way of enriching uranium uses centrifuges. A centrifuge is a machine that spins rapidly. As it spins, it throws the material inside it outward, separating lighter materials from heavier ones. Centrifuges can gradually separate the U-235 from the

U-238 until the uranium becomes enriched. Scientists are also experimenting with uranium enrichment using LASERS.

Escalation

Escalation is an increase in the level of tension or fighting between two countries. For example, suppose small groups of soldiers from neighboring countries have been fighting along their border. If one nation then attacks with tanks, or bombs the capital of the other, that would be an escalation.

Euromissiles

Euromissiles are Soviet and U.S. intermediate- and short-range MISSILES based in Europe. These include the U.S. PERSHING I AND II, LANCE, and CRUISE MISSILES, and the Soviet SS-20s.

Extremely Low Frequency (ELF)

Extremely low frequency (ELF) and very low frequency (VLF) radio waves are used to send messages to nuclear submarines. The United States sends information to its missile-launching submarines on several different very low and extremely low radio frequencies. Unlike ordinary radio waves, these signals can travel through water. The messages broadcast on these frequencies tell submarines whether or not to launch their MISSILES (see FAIL DEADLY).

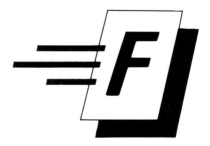

Fail-Deadly

Fail-deadly describes the method U.S. BALLISTIC MISSILE submarines use to know whether or not they should fire their nuclear MISSILES. The missiles on these submarines do not have the FAIL-SAFE locks that most land-based missiles and bombs do. Instead, the submarines receive regular messages on very low radio frequencies (see ELF). These messages tell them that everything above the surface is peaceful. Submarine commanders don't fire their missiles as long as they are receiving such signals.

In case of a nuclear war, these signals would stop. When the submarine no longer receives its signal, its first job is to try several other methods of getting messages from U.S. command posts. If the submarine *fails* to receive any messages, it then fires its *deadly* missiles at its targets.

Fail-Safe

Fail-safe describes an important safety feature of many NUCLEAR WEAPONS. Nuclear weapons are built so that if any of their systems *fails*, the weapon will remain in a *safe* condition. Fail-safe systems protect against accidental explosions. They also prevent someone who isn't supposed to have the weapon from exploding it. Fail-safe systems include an exact series of steps that must be followed before the nuclear weapon can be launched or exploded.

For example, to launch a MINUTEMAN nuclear MISSILE, two different Air Force officers must carry out a precise series of actions. The officers must use secret codes to arm the missile and prepare it for launching. They must also turn special keys, both at exactly the same time. If any of the steps is done incorrectly, the missile cannot be launched.

Many U.S. nuclear weapons have a fail-safe device called a PERMISSIVE ACTION LINK, or PAL. A PAL is an electronic lock. It will not allow a nuclear weapon to be fired unless the proper code is entered. Some PALs also permanently disarm the WARHEAD if the wrong code is used.

Not all U.S. nuclear weapons have PALs. However, they all have some safeguards to make it difficult to arm and fire them accidentally.

Fallout

Fallout is the rain of radioactive particles that falls from the sky after a nuclear explosion. A nuclear explosion carries huge amounts of radioactive matter into the air. Some fallout falls to earth quickly, near the BLAST. This is called local radioactive fallout. Other radioactive particles are carried many thousands of feet into the air and gradually drift back to earth. In the meantime, winds may carry the fallout thousands of miles from the explosion. This is known as delayed radioactive fallout.

Local fallout near a nuclear blast may contain enough RADIOACTIVITY to cause RADIATION SICKNESS or death. In addition to the immediate danger, even small amounts of delayed fallout contain radiation that may cause damage. Human beings take these particles into their bodies by breathing them or eating them in their food. Such radioactive elements may cause cancer years after a person was exposed to the fallout.

The danger from fallout depends on the particular circumstances through which people are exposed to it. Some NUCLEAR WEAPONS produce more radioactive fallout than others. Also, the radioactivity of fallout decreases fairly quickly as time passes. Two weeks after a nuclear explosion, only about one-thousandth of the original radioactivity will remain.

In the 1950s, above-ground nuclear tests such as this one created large amounts of radioactive fallout that spread around the world.

Some radioactive fallout, though, is long-lasting. For example, STRONTIUM 90, one of the elements in fallout, has a HALF-LIFE of twenty-eight years. After twenty-eight years, half of this radioactive material will still remain in the environment.

In the 1950s and early 1960s, Strontium 90 from nuclear tests was found in milk. It had fallen to earth and was eaten by cows. Parents worried that Strontium 90 was being absorbed into their children's bones and would cause cancer or other diseases.

Angry citizens staged many protests against fallout from nuclear testing. These protests helped persuade U.S. and Soviet government leaders to agree to the PARTIAL TEST BAN TREATY of 1963, which ended all above-ground NUCLEAR TESTS. Since that time, fallout from nuclear tests has been much less of a problem.

Fallout Shelter

A fallout shelter is a building designed to shield people from at least some of the radioactive FALLOUT from a nuclear explosion. A fallout shelter is usually built underground. It is stocked with enough food and water to last for days or weeks.

In the 1950s and 1960s, some people built fallout shelters in their basements. Others built underground shelters in their back yards. The U.S. government also set up shelters in the basements of some public buildings. Today, few Americans have well-supplied fallout shelters.

Fat Man

Fat Man was the nickname for the first PLUTO-NIUM bomb, which was built by the MANHATTAN PROJECT during World War II. It was called Fat Man because of its rounded shape. The bomb weighed about five tons (4.5 metric tons). It was dropped over NAGASAKI, Japan, on August 9, 1945.

Fat Man was an IMPLOSION bomb. Such bombs work by squeezing a small amount of plutonium into a CRITICAL MASS with high explosives (see FISSION WARHEAD).

Federal Emergency Management Agency (FEMA)

The Federal Emergency Management Agency (FEMA) is the part of the U.S. government that is in charge of CIVIL DEFENSE. FEMA makes plans for such disasters as a nuclear attack, as well as floods, earthquakes, and other natural disasters. It also teaches people how to protect themselves from the dangers of these disasters.

In the past few years, FEMA has been criticized for making plans that may not work. FEMA's critics think it is foolish to plan to evacuate millions of people from U.S. cities in time to escape from a nuclear attack. They think it is foolish to plan for mail delivery and land ownership after a nuclear war. Yet others think it is foolish not to plan ahead, even though a nuclear war would destroy much of the country.

Fermi, Enrico (1901-1954)

Enrico Fermi was an Italian-born physicist who carried out scientific experiments that led to the development of the first ATOMIC BOMB. Fermi was the first to discover that a nuclear CHAIN REACTION was possible. He created the first chain reaction in a NUCLEAR REACTOR in 1942. The U.S. government then built other nuclear reactors to make enough PLUTONIUM for atomic bombs.

Enrico Fermi demonstrates a scientific principle related to his work.

Fireball

A fireball is the huge, hot ball of gases formed by a nuclear explosion. The fireball from a one-MEGATON nuclear BLAST may be more than a mile (nearly two kilometers) across. Temperatures in the center of the fireball reach millions of degrees. As the fireball rises into the atmosphere, it forms a mushroom-shaped cloud.

Firestorm

A firestorm is a huge fire covering a large area of land. It sucks in large amounts of oxygen from the surrounding air, creating fierce winds and flames that may be thousands of feet high. Firestorms are deadly because of their heat and their winds. They also use up so much oxygen that there is not enough left for people to breathe. A nuclear attack on a city would probably create a firestorm.

First Strike

A first strike is a nuclear attack on an enemy before the enemy has a chance to attack with its nuclear forces. A first strike is sometimes called a PREEMPTIVE ATTACK.

First Use

First use refers to the nation that is the first to use NUCLEAR WEAPONS during a war.

Fissile Material

Fissile material refers to radioactive metals such as PLUTONIUM 239 or URANIUM 235 that can be used to fuel a NUCLEAR BOMB or NUCLEAR REACTOR. This material is called "fissile" because its ATOMS can be made to split — the process of FISSION. Uranium 233 is also fissile, but it is not used in NUCLEAR WEAPONS or reactors.

Fission

Fission is the nuclear reaction that provides the energy for URANIUM and PLUTONIUM bombs, and for NUCLEAR REACTORS. Fission, which means "splitting apart," is sometimes known as "splitting the ATOM."

Fission starts when the NUCLEUS of a uranium or plutonium atom is struck by a NEUTRON (a tiny atomic particle). This causes the nucleus to split into two or more pieces. It also releases energy in the form of light, heat, gamma rays, and atomic particles — including more neutrons.

If there is enough uranium or plutonium in one place (a CRITICAL MASS), the neutrons from one fission will strike other atoms and cause more fission. It is this CHAIN REACTION that creates the explosion of a fission bomb, or the power in a nuclear reactor.

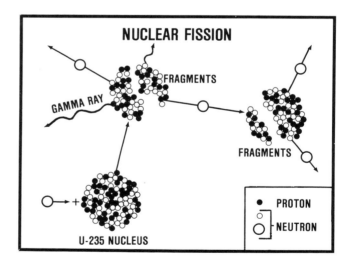

NUCLEAR FISSION

GAMMA RAY

FRAGMENTS

FRAGMENTS

U-235 NUCLEUS

● PROTON
○ NEUTRON

Fission Warhead

A fission warhead is a nuclear explosive fueled by the FISSION of PLUTONIUM 239 or URANIUM 235. Fission warheads are commonly known as "ATOMIC BOMBS."

In a modern fission warhead, a few pounds of plutonium form a hollow sphere. At the center of the sphere is a source of NEUTRONS called the "initiator." The sphere is surrounded by a shell of material which reflects neutrons back into the center, where the CHAIN REACTION takes place. Non-nuclear high explosives surround the shell.

When the high explosives fire, they squeeze the nuclear fuel into a much smaller area, creating a CRITICAL MASS. A critical mass is the amount and density of nuclear fuel needed to create a chain reaction. At the same time, the initiator and an electronic device called a "neutron trigger" give off bursts of neutrons. These set off a rapid chain reaction, and create the nuclear explosion.

Because the explosives in a fission warhead are focused inward to squeeze the uranium or plutonium together, this type of nuclear WARHEAD is sometimes called an "IMPLOSION bomb."

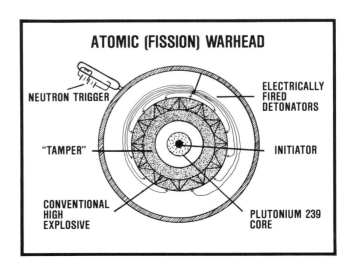

ATOMIC (FISSION) WARHEAD

NEUTRON TRIGGER

ELECTRICALLY FIRED DETONATORS

"TAMPER"

INITIATOR

CONVENTIONAL HIGH EXPLOSIVE

PLUTONIUM 239 CORE

Fixed Launcher

A fixed launcher is a MISSILE launcher that stays in one place. An underground MISSILE SILO is an example of a fixed launcher.

Flexible Response

Flexible response is the name of a U.S. nuclear STRATEGY which began in the early 1960s. It was first announced as a policy by the Kennedy administration.

Flexible response means the United States can respond to an attack by the Soviet Union or some other country in a variety of ways. If the United States were attacked by conventional (non-nuclear) forces, it would defend itself with conventional forces of its own. It would respond to attacks by "small" tactical NUCLEAR WEAPONS with similar weapons.

The idea of flexible response took the place of "MASSIVE RETALIATION," the U.S. strategy of the 1950s. Massive retaliation meant responding to any kind of Soviet attack with an all-out nuclear attack. Flexible response is a term used by President Reagan to describe U.S. nuclear strategy in the 1980s.

Flight Test

A flight test is the test of a MISSILE, CRUISE MISSILE, or other flying weapon. Flight tests of nuclear missiles are now carried out with dummy WARHEADS. In the 1950s and early 1960s, some missiles were tested with actual nuclear warheads. However, the PARTIAL TEST BAN TREATY of 1963 no longer allows such tests.

Football

Football is the slang term for the briefcase of nuclear codes and plans that the U.S. president would use in time of war. The football is carried and guarded by a military aide. It is kept near the president at all times.

Fratricide

Fratricide means killing a brother. In military terms, it means that the explosion of one nuclear WARHEAD may damage or destroy "brother" warheads that are attacking the same target.

Fratricide would be most likely to happen in an attack on HARD TARGETS such as MISSILE SILOS. Since hard targets must be hit almost directly to be destroyed, several warheads are aimed at each target. If the warheads reach the target at about the same time, the first explosion could damage the other warheads or throw them off course.

Fuel Cycle

The fuel cycle is the series of steps required to produce, use, and reprocess fuel for NUCLEAR REACTORS. The complete nuclear fuel cycle includes these steps: mining and enriching URANIUM; turning the uranium into reactor fuel rods; REPROCESSING the used fuel rods, recycling the unused fuel; and getting rid of the nuclear waste.

The nuclear fuel cycle produces large amounts of PLUTONIUM as a waste product. This heavy, radioactive metal can be used as fuel for NUCLEAR WEAPONS.

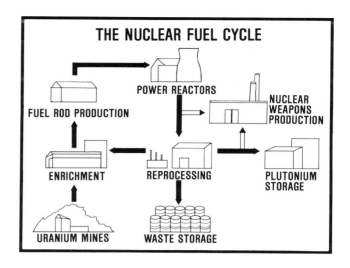

THE NUCLEAR FUEL CYCLE

POWER REACTORS

NUCLEAR WEAPONS PRODUCTION

FUEL ROD PRODUCTION

ENRICHMENT

REPROCESSING

PLUTONIUM STORAGE

URANIUM MINES

WASTE STORAGE

Fusion

Fusion is a nuclear reaction. In a fusion reaction, the NUCLEI of two small ATOMS join together, or fuse, to form one larger atomic NUCLEUS. This reaction releases large amounts of energy — much more energy than a fission reaction using the same amount of material.

The energy of the sun and other stars is produced by fusion. Fusion also occurs in a thermonuclear or hydrogen WARHEAD. Scientists are experimenting with ways to control fusion reactions to make electricity.

THERMONUCLEAR WEAPONS use special ISOTOPES (varieties) of hydrogen called DEUTERIUM and TRITIUM. In a thermonuclear explosion, two atoms of hydrogen combine to form one helium atom. This fusion creates tremendous amounts of heat, light, and other RADIATION.

Fusion occurs only under extremely high temperature and pressure. A nuclear fission explosion fueled with URANIUM or PLUTONIUM is needed to start the fusion reaction in a thermonuclear warhead.

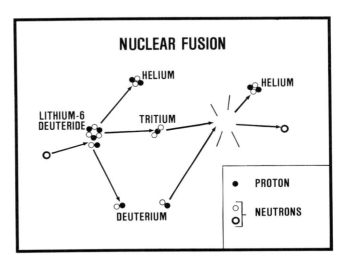

Fusion Warhead (see THERMONUCLEAR WEAPON)

Gamma Radiation

Gamma radiation is a kind of RADIATION given off by radioactive elements. Gamma rays are high-energy electromagnetic waves, very much like X RAYS. They have no weight and no electrical charge. Large amounts of gamma rays are created by nuclear explosions.

Gamma rays travel at the speed of light (186,000 miles or 300,000 kilometers per second). Like light, they can travel great distances. Gamma rays are powerful enough to pass through more than an inch (about three centimeters) of steel. They can easily pass through human flesh and damage the human body. Gamma rays are much more powerful than ALPHA or BETA RADIATION.

George Shot

The George Shot was the code name of a U.S. NUCLEAR TEST that took place on May 8, 1951, on ENIWETOK ATOLL in the South Pacific Ocean. The George Shot was the first test of a thermonuclear (FUSION) explosion. It was not an actual weapon, but it did prove that hydrogen bombs were possible.

Government Owned - Contractor Operated

Many large U.S. companies are involved in making NUCLEAR WEAPONS. The U.S. government owns large factories that make nuclear weapons and their parts. The government also owns nuclear weapons research laboratories. Private contractors (companies) run many of these factories and labs.

For example, the SAVANNAH RIVER PLANT produces all U.S. PLUTONIUM. It is operated by the DuPont company. The Martin-Marietta company runs the OAK RIDGE factory that makes THERMONUCLEAR WEAPONS parts. And the University of California runs the LAWRENCE LIVERMORE NATIONAL LABORATORY, where nuclear weapons are designed.

Ground Burst

A NUCLEAR WEAPON that explodes at ground level is called a ground burst. A ground burst digs a deep crater in the earth. It also throws many tons of radioactive dust into the atmosphere. In a war, ground bursts would be used to destroy targets that are buried underground or protected with heavy concrete and steel.

Ground Wave Emergency Network (GWEN)

The Ground Wave Emergency Network (GWEN) is a U.S. radio communications system designed to carry messages during a nuclear war. Hundreds of GWEN radio towers are located throughout the United States and Canada.

Ground Zero

Ground zero is the point on the earth's surface directly beneath a nuclear explosion.

Groves, General Leslie R.

General Leslie Groves was the U.S. Army commander in charge of the MANHATTAN PROJECT during World War II. The Manhattan Project was the U.S. research program that built the first NUCLEAR BOMBS. Groves is also known as the commander who supervised the building of the PENTAGON (DEPARTMENT OF DEFENSE headquarters).

Groves was a construction engineer, not a scientist. He made sure that all the factories and laboratories needed for the program were built quickly and correctly. He was also responsible for keeping the Manhattan Project a secret.

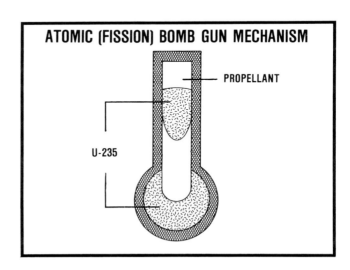

ATOMIC (FISSION) BOMB GUN MECHANISM

PROPELLANT

U-235

Gun Mechanism

The first NUCLEAR BOMB was designed in the form of a gun. Two pieces of URANIUM were placed at opposite ends of a long tube. Neither chunk of uranium was large enough to form a CRITICAL MASS and explode. To explode the bomb, one of the uranium chunks was fired into the other. Together, they formed a single piece of uranium big enough to start a CHAIN REACTION and explode.

The nuclear bomb dropped on HIROSHIMA, Japan, was designed in this way. It was probably the only nuclear bomb ever built using a gun mechanism. All other NUCLEAR WEAPONS have been IMPLOSION weapons (see FISSION WARHEAD).

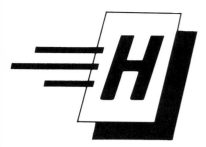

Half-Life

Half-life is the length of time it takes for one-half of a radioactive substance to change into other substances through RADIOACTIVE DECAY. Often a half-life is also the time it takes for that substance to lose one-half of its RADIOACTIVITY.

For example, iodine 131 is a radioactive ISOTOPE (variety) of iodine. It has a half-life of about eight days. Suppose a sample of iodine 131 was releasing ten units of RADIATION today. After eight days it will produce just five units. The rest of the iodine 131 will have changed into other non-radioactive substances. Eight days after that, it will have lost another half of its radioactivity.

Each radioactive isotope has a different half-life. Some half-lives are very short. For example, carbon 11 has a half-life of just twenty minutes, and radon 222 has a half-life of about four days. Other substances stay radioactive for extremely long times. PLUTONIUM 239 has a half-life of 24,100 years, and URANIUM 238 has a half-life of 4.5 billion years.

Hanford Reservation, Washington

Hanford Reservation is a huge area of U.S. government land in southeastern Washington state. It has been used for NUCLEAR WEAPONS manufacturing since 1943. The PLUTONIUM used in the first ATOMIC BOMBS was made at Hanford. The Hanford plant still has reactors that can produce plutonium, and factories to purify the plutonium. However, these factories are no longer operating. All the plutonium for U.S. weapons is now produced at the SAVANNAH RIVER PLANT in South Carolina.

Hanford also has a huge dump for nuclear waste where most high-level waste from U.S. nuclear weapons production is stored. Some of this highly RADIOACTIVE WASTE has leaked into the ground, causing difficult and expensive problems. Large amounts of RADIOACTIVITY have also been released into the atmosphere from Hanford reactors. Hanford has been suggested as the first U.S. location for deep, permanent burial of high-level nuclear waste.

Hardened Silo

A hardened silo is a MISSILE launching tube buried in the ground. It is covered by huge steel and concrete doors. The earth, steel, and concrete that surrounds the missile protects it from almost any attack. A hardened silo can be destroyed only by a direct hit from a nuclear WARHEAD.

Hard Target

A hard target is a military target built to withstand any attack except a direct hit by a nuclear WARHEAD. Targets are "hardened" when they are built underground, and sealed with massive steel and concrete doors. Some military command centers are hard targets, as well as the MISSILE SILOS where the United States and the Soviet Union keep their land-based MISSILES.

H-Bomb (see THERMONUCLEAR WEAPON)

Heavy Hydrogen

Heavy hydrogen is another term for DEUTE-RIUM.

Heavy Water

Heavy water is water that contains high levels of DEUTERIUM, often called "heavy hydrogen." Deuterium is a fuel for THERMONUCLEAR WEAPONS (hydrogen bombs).

Hydrogen itself is an extremely light gas which is difficult to use. But hydrogen is also found in water. Water molecules are made up of two hydrogen ATOMS and one oxygen atom. Because water is easy to work with, deuterium is often stored and handled in liquid form, known as heavy water.

Heavy water is made from ordinary water. A small percentage of water molecules contains deuterium atoms. These water molecules are separated from ordinary water by distillation or other methods.

Heavy water is also used in some production reactors — NUCLEAR REACTORS that make PLUTONIUM. The plutonium is then used in nuclear WARHEADS or power reactors.

High-Level Nuclear Waste

High-level nuclear waste refers to the waste products produced in making weapons-grade PLUTONIUM or URANIUM. High-level waste also comes from REPROCESSING the fuel from NUCLEAR REACTORS.

High-level waste is highly radioactive and very dangerous. It is difficult to handle because it creates so much heat. This type of waste is often stored in tanks as liquid or sludge.

The U.S. government plans to build a permanent burial site for high-level nuclear waste by the late 1990s. In the meantime, the waste is stored at HANFORD, WASHINGTON, and the SAVANNAH RIVER PLANT in South Carolina.

Hiroshima

Hiroshima is a city in southwestern Japan, on the island of Honshu. It was destroyed by the first ATOMIC BOMB to be used in warfare. On August 6, 1945, a U.S. B-29 bomber dropped a URANIUM bomb on Hiroshima. The explosion, which had a force equal to about 13,000 tons of TNT, killed almost 100,000 people. Thousands of victims were killed instantly by the heat and BLAST of the explosion. Many others died days or months later from burns and RADIATION poisoning. Still others died years afterward from leukemia or other cancers.

Hiroshima has been rebuilt, and it is now a thriving city of nearly a million people. Hiroshima Peace Park was built near the center of the city, where the bomb exploded. The park is a memorial to all who died in the nuclear explosion, and a reminder to people everywhere of the enormous destructive power of NUCLEAR WEAPONS.

This building in Hiroshima, Japan, became a monument after the end of World War II. It was one of the few buildings left standing in the city when this photograph was taken in September 1945.

Homeporting

Homeporting is the U.S. Navy plan that bases nuclear-armed warships in several new port cities, including New York and San Francisco. The purpose of homeporting is to spread out the U.S. fleet to make it harder to destroy in an enemy attack. The U.S. government also believes that spreading out the fleet will make it better prepared to respond to military emergencies.

Many people in the new cities have opposed the plan. They don't want nuclear weapons stored near their homes, and they believe that homeporting turns their cities into military targets.

Homing

Homing means finding a target. A MISSILE may use computers, RADAR, radio, or heat sensors to home in on its target.

Hot Launch

A hot launch is a method of launching a MISSILE from an underground silo or a missile tube on a submarine. In a hot launch, the rocket engines fire inside the silo or tube. The engines force the missile out of the launching tube and send it on its way. Since the heat and BLAST of the engines damage the launcher, it cannot be reused without major repairs (see COLD LAUNCH).

Hotline

The hotline is a communications system that connects the U.S. and Soviet governments. It can send information between Washington, D.C., and Moscow in times of crisis. Such a system of rapid communication may prevent misunderstandings that could lead to nuclear war.

The two countries established the hotline in 1963, after the CUBAN MISSILE CRISIS. Since then, they improved the system in 1971 and 1975. In September 1987, the United States and the Soviet Union signed the Nuclear Risk Reduction Agreement, in which they agreed to make more improvements in the hotline. The new, computerized hotline will be able to carry much more information, and display it more quickly.

Hydrogen Bomb (see THERMONUCLEAR WEAPON)

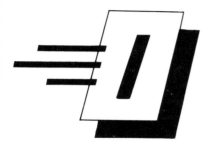

ICBM (see INTERCONTINENTAL BALLISTIC MISSILE)

Implosion

An implosion is an explosion that is directed inward. In a nuclear WARHEAD, the nuclear fuel is squeezed into a CRITICAL MASS by an implosion of non-nuclear high explosives (see FISSION WARHEAD).

INF (see INTERMEDIATE NUCLEAR FORCE)

INF Treaty

The INF Treaty is a proposed TREATY between the United States and the Soviet Union that would eliminate all intermediate-range missiles belonging to both countries. The two nations agreed to this plan—also known as the double zero or ZERO OPTION—in September 1987.

Intercontinental

Intercontinental refers to the ability to travel between continents. It is used to describe large MISSILES able to hit targets on another continent. It also describes bombers that have the range to fly between continents.

The United States is located on the continent of North America. The Soviet Union is located on the continents of Europe and Asia. Any weapon that can travel between these two countries is considered intercontinental. Intercontinental weapons are also known as STRATEGIC WEAPONS.

Intercontinental Ballistic Missile (ICBM)

An intercontinental ballistic missile (ICBM) is a MISSILE that can launch nuclear WARHEADS over distances of thousands of miles. Most modern ICBMs are based in underground launch pads called silos. Others are based on MOBILE LAUNCHERS — heavy vehicles which can move the missiles from place to place.

Modern ICBMs do not have to be filled with fuel before they are fired. They burn solid fuel that is permanently stored in the missile. These missiles are ready to be fired at any time, with just a moment's notice. Many modern ICBMs carry more than one warhead. Such warheads are called MULTIPLE INDEPENDENTLY TARGETABLE REENTRY VEHICLES, or MIRVS.

The U.S. ICBM force includes MINUTEMAN II and MINUTEMAN III MISSILES, and the new MX missile. The United States has more than 1,000 land-based ICBMs, which carry more than 2,000 warheads. The total YIELD of these warheads is about 1,600 MEGATONS of explosive power. U.S. ICBMs are based in several western and midwestern states, including Arizona, Arkansas, Colorado, Kansas, Missouri, Montana, and North and South Dakota.

The Soviet Union has about 1,400 ICBMs. Soviet ICBMs are known by the letters *SS* followed by a number (SS-18, for example — see SS MISSILE). Soviet ICBMs carry about 4,000 warheads, and their total yield is probably more than 7,000 megatons. The French and Chinese have smaller numbers of ICBMs.

ICBMs are only one part of Soviet and U.S. strategic nuclear forces. Both countries also have long-range bombers, SUBMARINE-LAUNCHED BALLISTIC MISSILES, and many shorter-range NUCLEAR WEAPONS.

Intermediate Nuclear Force (INF)

Intermediate nuclear forces (INF) are NU-CLEAR WEAPONS of medium range. They include weapons with ranges from about 300 miles (483 kilometers) to about 3,400 miles (5,474 kilometers). U.S. weapons in this category are PERSHING II and CRUISE MISSILES, as well as medium-range bombers such as the FB-111. Most U.S. and Soviet INF weapons are based in Europe.

There is no standard way to distinguish intermediate-range weapons from STRATEGIC (long-range) WEAPONS. In fact, INF weapons are included in Soviet and U.S. strategic planning. Yet in ARMS CONTROL talks, the United States and the Soviet Union have separated INF weapons from strategic weapons. Because intermediate-range weapons have a shorter range than strategic weapons, they are better suited for use within a geographic region than for an intercontinental nuclear attack. In September 1987, the United States and the Soviet Union reached an agreement in principle to eliminate their INTERMEDIATE-RANGE BALLISTIC MISSILES and ground-launched CRUISE MISSILES.

Intermediate-Range Ballistic Missile (IRBM)

An intermediate-range ballistic missile (IRBM) is a MISSILE that can launch one or more nuclear WARHEADS over a distance from about 300 miles (483 kilometers) to 3,400 miles (5,474 kilometers). The U.S. IRBM force consists of PERSHING II missiles. The main Soviet IRBM is known as the SS-20 (see SS MISSILE).

Intermediate-Range Bomber

An intermediate-range bomber is an airplane that can carry nuclear or non-nuclear bombs and MISSILES over a distance of as far as several thousand miles. The FB-111 is the U.S. intermediate-range bomber. The Soviet "Backfire" bomber may be considered either an intermediate or a strategic (long-range) aircraft.

International Atomic Energy Agency (IAEA)

The International Atomic Energy Agency (IAEA) was created in 1956 as a branch of the United Nations. In 1968 when the NUCLEAR NON-PROLIFERATION TREATY was signed, the participating nations agreed to let the IAEA supervise NUCLEAR ENERGY programs around the world. The agency checks nuclear power plants to make sure they follow safety rules. It also tries to make sure that nuclear materials are safeguarded.

Even though the IAEA attempts to prevent the spread of NUCLEAR WEAPONS, it has very little power to make nations follow its rules. It can warn the world if a country begins to develop nuclear weapons. A few nations, including Pakistan, India, Israel, and South Africa, do not allow the IAEA to inspect their nuclear activities. All these countries have, or will soon have, their own nuclear weapons.

Ionizing Radiation

An ATOM that loses one or more ELECTRONS is called an ion. Ionizing radiation is any kind of RADIATION strong enough to knock electrons off the atoms it strikes. X RAYS, gamma rays, NEUTRONS, and alpha and beta particles are all forms of ionizing radiation.

Ionizing radiation is produced in nuclear reactions, including nuclear explosions. It is also given off by naturally radioactive elements, and by radioactive FALLOUT. Such radiation can harm humans and animals by ionizing atoms in the body. This changes the chemical makeup of cells, causing RADIATION SICKNESS and cancer.

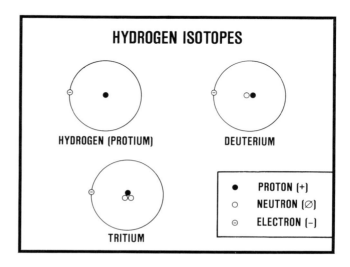

HYDROGEN ISOTOPES

HYDROGEN (PROTIUM)　　DEUTERIUM

TRITIUM

●	PROTON (+)
○	NEUTRON (∅)
⊖	ELECTRON (−)

Isotope

An isotope is one of several different varieties of a chemical element. Each isotope has the same number of PROTONS and ELECTRONS. The only difference among isotopes is the number of NEUTRONS in the NUCLEUS.

All the isotopes of a single element have the same chemical properties. However, some isotopes of each element are stable, while others may be radioactive. For example, hydrogen has three different isotopes. Ordinary hydrogen has one proton and no neutrons in its nucleus. DEUTERIUM has one proton and one neutron, and TRITIUM has one proton and two neutrons. Tritium is radioactive, but the other two isotopes of hydrogen are not.

Isotopes are named with the chemical symbol for the element, followed by the total number of protons and neutrons in the nucleus. For example, U-235 is one isotope of URANIUM. U-235 has 92 protons and 143 neutrons in its nucleus. U-238, the most common isotope of uranium, has 92 protons and 146 neutrons.

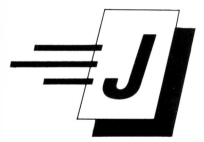

Joe 1 Nuclear Test

Joe 1 was the U.S. name for the first Soviet NUCLEAR TEST, which took place on August 29, 1949. It was given the name Joe because the Soviet leader at the time was Josef Stalin. The first Soviet test took the U.S. government and the rest of the world by surprise. Before that time, most people had thought the United States would be the only country to have NUCLEAR WEAPONS for many years.

Joe 4 Nuclear Test

Joe 4 was the U.S. name for the first Soviet test of a thermonuclear (hydrogen) explosion, which occurred on August 12, 1953. It, too, was named after the Soviet leader, Josef Stalin. The Joe 4 test showed that the United States would not be the only country to have THERMONUCLEAR WEAPONS.

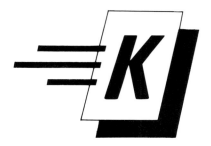

Kiloton

A kiloton is a unit used to measure the size of an atomic explosion. The prefix *kilo* means 1,000 and one kiloton is an explosion equal to 1,000 tons of TNT. Nuclear WARHEADS range from a few kilotons to several thousand kilotons in explosive power (see MEGATON).

Kinetic Energy Weapon

Kinetic energy is the energy of motion. A kinetic energy weapon is one that shoots extremely fast moving objects at its target. Such a weapon does not need an explosive WARHEAD because the speed of the object is enough to shatter and destroy the target.

The United States has tested a small anti-satellite missile that destroys its target in this way. If and when they are developed, RAIL GUNS will also be kinetic energy weapons.

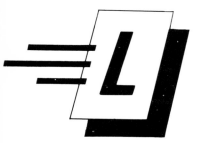

Lance

The Lance is a U.S. SHORT-RANGE BALLISTIC MISSILE with a range of 78 miles (125 kilometers).

Laser

The word *laser* stands for Light Amplification by Stimulated Emission of Radiation. A laser is a tightly focused beam of light, all of a single wavelength. A laser beam travels at the speed of light, 186,000 miles (300,000 kilometers) per second. Some lasers have very low power, while others have enough energy to cut through steel.

Lasers have many uses in science, industry, and medicine. Military researchers are also experimenting with ways to use lasers as weapons. The Reagan administration's STRATEGIC DEFENSE INITIATIVE ("Star Wars") includes plans to use laser weapons to shoot down enemy MISSILES. These weapons have not yet been built or tested.

Launcher

A launcher is a device that supports a MISSILE until it is fired. Some missile launchers are mobile — they can move from place to place. Others are "fixed" — they stay in one permanent location. Underground MISSILE SILOS are examples of FIXED LAUNCHERS.

Launch on Impact

Launch on impact is a plan to launch nuclear MISSILES against an enemy only after the enemy's first missiles have exploded. A country with a launch on impact plan would be certain it was being attacked before it fired back. As a result, that nation would be less likely to launch its missiles by mistake. However, a country using this plan risks losing some of its weapons in a FIRST STRIKE by an enemy.

Launch on Warning

Launch on warning is a plan to launch a country's nuclear MISSILES as soon as RADAR or satellites warn of an enemy's nuclear attack. Launch on warning places a country's nuclear forces on a hair-trigger alert. At the first sign of an attack, missiles would be launched.

Most people agree that a launch on warning policy is quite dangerous and could cause a nuclear war to start by accident. Radar and satellite warning systems often give false alarms. Several minutes or more may pass before these false warnings are corrected. But if missiles are launched on warning, a false alarm could result in a launch, and a nuclear war.

Both the U.S. and the Soviet governments claim they do not have a launch on warning policy now. The Soviets threatened to use such a policy in 1983, when the United States began to DEPLOY PERSHING II missiles in Europe. Pershing IIs can reach Soviet territory in just six minutes. Suppose Soviet radars warn of an attack. In such a situation, Soviet leaders would have very little time to decide if they were faced with a real or a false alarm. They might decide to launch missiles automatically, as soon as they received warning of an attack.

Launch Under Attack

Launch under attack refers to the military plan for a country to launch nuclear MISSILES only when it is sure enemy missiles are attacking. In a launch under attack plan, a nation would prepare to launch its missiles when RADAR and satellites warned that enemy missiles had been fired. But it would not actually launch until there was definite proof that the enemy was attacking.

Both the United States and the Soviet Union currently have a policy of launching only under attack. That means neither country will launch its nuclear missiles unless it is attacked first. This policy is not in effect for U.S. forces in Europe, however (see NO FIRST USE). A launch under attack policy makes accidental nuclear war less likely than LAUNCH ON WARNING.

Lawrence, Ernest O. (1901-1958)

Ernest O. Lawrence was a nuclear scientist who worked on the MANHATTAN PROJECT. Lawrence is best known as the inventor of the cyclotron, an "atom-smashing" machine that allowed scientists to study atomic structure.

Lawrence tried, unsuccessfully, to use the cyclotron to make enriched URANIUM for NUCLEAR BOMBS. In the late 1940s, Lawrence was a strong supporter of plans to build THERMONUCLEAR (hydrogen) WEAPONS.

Lawrence Livermore National Laboratory

Lawrence Livermore National Laboratory in Livermore, California, is one of three U.S. NUCLEAR WEAPONS laboratories (the others are LOS ALAMOS and SANDIA in New Mexico. It is named in honor of the nuclear scientist ERNEST O. LAWRENCE. Lawrence Livermore National Laboratory is run by the University of California. Its scientists carry out research on how nuclear weapons work, and design new weapons. They also perform research on LASERS, FUSION power, and other physics problems.

Layered Defense

A layered defense is part of the proposed plans for the STRATEGIC DEFENSE INITIATIVE ("Star Wars"). In this plan, the United States would have a series (layers) of antimissile weapons.

The first layer would be satellites that could track and shoot down enemy MISSILES as they are launched. A second layer would destroy the missiles' WARHEADS as they glided above the atmosphere. A third layer, consisting of ANTIBALLISTIC MISSILES (ABMS) and other ground-based weapons, would shoot down incoming warheads as they headed for their targets.

At this time, a layered defense is only an

idea — the weapons for such a defense do not yet exist. Some scientists doubt that such a defense could ever work effectively. Others think that a layered defense might be built, if the United States spends enough on research.

Limited Test Ban Treaty (see PARTIAL TEST BAN TREATY)

Limited (Nuclear) War

Limited war refers to a war in which limited numbers of NUCLEAR WEAPONS are used. The STRATEGY of limited war involves the use of a few nuclear weapons to convince an enemy to cease fighting.

Many people believe that a limited nuclear war between the United States and the Soviet Union could not be controlled. Instead, they say, such a conflict would probably become an all-out war in which both sides would be completely destroyed.

Liquid Fuel

Liquid fuel is a type of fuel that was used in early INTERCONTINENTAL BALLISTIC MISSILES. It is difficult, and sometimes dangerous, to store liquid fuel in MISSILES. Instead, fuel tanks had to be filled just before the weapon was ready to be fired. Because this process took hours, the missile could not be fired on short notice.

The United States now uses SOLID FUEL in all its missiles. Since solid fuel can be stored in a missile for long periods of time, the missile is ready to be fired on a moment's notice. Some Soviet missiles such as the SS-18 still use liquid fuel, although many other Soviet missiles now use solid fuel.

Lithium

Lithium is an extremely light metallic element. Combined with DEUTERIUM (heavy hydrogen), it is used as the fuel for THERMO-NUCLEAR (hydrogen) WEAPONS.

Lithium Deuteride

Lithium deuteride is a chemical compound made of LITHIUM and DEUTERIUM (heavy hydrogen). It is the FUSION fuel in modern thermonuclear (hydrogen) WARHEADS. Lithium deuteride, a gray, powdery material, is the most convenient form of fusion fuel for THERMONUCLEAR WEAPONS. It is easier to handle than either hydrogen gas or liquid water, which also contains hydrogen.

In a thermonuclear explosion, the lithium changes into TRITIUM. The tritium and deuterium then fuse (join together), releasing tremendous amounts of energy.

Little Boy

Little Boy was the nickname given to the first URANIUM bomb built by the MANHATTAN PROJECT in 1945. Built in the shape of a cylinder, the bomb was about ten feet (three meters) long and weighed about 9,000 pounds (4,100 kilograms).

Scientists of the Manhattan Project had only enough uranium to build one such bomb. They were so sure their design would work that they didn't test it. Little Boy was dropped on the Japanese city of HIROSHIMA on August 6, 1945. The resulting BLAST leveled the city and killed about 100,000 people.

The "Little Boy" bomb that destroyed the city of Hiroshima, Japan, looked much like this later atomic bomb.

Local Radioactive Fallout

Local radioactive fallout is the radioactive dust from a nuclear explosion that falls back to earth soon after the BLAST. Local fallout lands near the site of the explosion, and can cause serious RADIATION SICKNESS (see FALLOUT).

Long-Range Bomber (see STRATEGIC BOMBER)

Lop Nor

Lop Nor, located in western China, is the test site for most Chinese NUCLEAR WEAPONS.

Los Alamos

Los Alamos was the first U.S. NUCLEAR WEAPONS laboratory. Located in New Mexico, near Santa Fe, Los Alamos was the main laboratory for the MANHATTAN PROJECT during World War II. The world's first NUCLEAR BOMBS were designed and built there.

Los Alamos is now one of the three U.S. nuclear weapons laboratories. (SANDIA in New Mexico and LAWRENCE LIVERMORE in California are the others.) The Los Alamos National

Laboratory is run by the University of California. Scientists at Los Alamos carry out research on how nuclear weapons work, and design new weapons.

Los Alamos National Laboratory in New Mexico served as the center for the development of the atomic bomb by the Manhattan Project scientists.

Low-Altitude Defense System (LOADS)

A low-altitude defense system (LOADS) refers to an antimissile defense that would destroy incoming WARHEADS in the last few seconds before they struck their targets. Such a system would probably use small, fast MISSILES and beam weapons such as LASERS.

Neither the United States nor the Soviet Union now has a LOADS defense. This type of defense is not allowed by the ABM TREATY. However, a LOADS defense might be developed and tested as part of the Reagan administration's STRATEGIC DEFENSE INITIATIVE ("Star Wars").

Low-Level Nuclear Waste

Low-level nuclear waste includes a wide range of radioactive materials. Most low-level waste comes from nuclear power plants. Other low-level waste comes from medical and industrial uses of radioactive materials.

Despite its name, some low-level waste can be highly radioactive and dangerous. Most low-level wastes, though, have fairly short HALF-LIVES. They may stay dangerous for months, or years. In comparison, high-level waste remains dangerous for thousands of years.

U.S. low-level radioactive waste is now buried at several sites around the country. In recent years, some states have complained about having to bury low-level wastes from other states. The United States is now developing a nationwide plan for disposing of low-level waste.

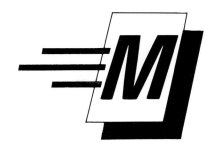

MAD (see MUTUALLY ASSURED DESTRUCTION)

Maneuverable Reentry Vehicle (MARV)

A maneuverable reentry vehicle (MARV) is a MISSILE WARHEAD that can change its course as it approaches its target. The United States is now developing MARV warheads, but none have yet been placed on U.S. missiles. The guidance system of a MARV will make it more accurate than other missiles. Such a system may also help the warhead avoid antimissile defenses.

Manhattan Project

The Manhattan Project was the name of the World War II program that built the first ATOMIC BOMB. The program began in 1940 after a group of well-known scientists warned President Franklin Roosevelt that Nazi Germany might be working on a NUCLEAR BOMB. Roosevelt decided to start a U.S. nuclear research program. Full-scale work on the project began in 1942.

The Manhattan Project was directed by DR. J. ROBERT OPPENHEIMER. Many of the greatest scientists of the time — ENRICO FERMI, HANS BETHE, ERNEST LAWRENCE, EDWARD TELLER, and LEO SZILARD — worked with him on the project. Most of the work was done at a laboratory in LOS ALAMOS, New Mexico.

At the time, the Manhattan Project was the most expensive and complicated scientific project ever attempted. Building a nuclear bomb was extremely difficult. First, many scientific problems had to be solved. Factories had to be built to enrich URANIUM, to produce PLUTONIUM, and to construct other bomb parts. All the scientific facts about NUCLEAR WEAPONS had to be discovered as the work progressed, and everything had to be kept top secret.

The scientists at Los Alamos designed two different kinds of bombs. One was armed with uranium, and the other used plutonium. On July 16, 1945, the Manhattan Project tested its first plutonium bomb in the New Mexico desert in a test Oppenheimer called "Trinity." The Trinity bomb exploded successfully.

By that time, Germany had surrendered, but the United States was still at war with

Workers from the Manhattan Project prepare the site for the Trinity atomic bomb test in the New Mexico desert in 1945.

Japan. The Manhattan Project scientists built two more bombs. Some of the scientists didn't want to use the bombs against Japan. Instead, they wanted to demonstrate the power of the bomb in the desert in an effort to convince Japan to surrender. President Truman, however, decided to use the two bombs against Japanese targets.

On August 6, 1945, the first bomb destroyed the city of HIROSHIMA. Three days later, the second bomb was dropped on the city of NAGASAKI. The two bombs killed about 150,000 people. Japan surrendered on August 14.

Massive Retaliation

Massive retaliation was the name of the U.S. nuclear STRATEGY in the 1950s. It was made the official U.S. policy by the Eisenhower administration in 1954. Massive retaliation was the U.S. threat to use an all-out nuclear attack against the Soviet Union, if the Soviets attacked the United States or its allies. At this time, the United States had many more NUCLEAR WEAPONS than the Soviet Union. The threat of massive retaliation was used mainly to warn the Soviets against attacking western Europe.

Medical Effects Of Nuclear War

A nuclear explosion has many disastrous medical effects. These effects on human life include:

Blast injuries. A nuclear explosion creates a powerful shock wave, and winds as high as 600 miles (966 kilometers) per hour. The shock wave from a one-MEGATON explosion is powerful enough to kill almost everyone within five miles (eight kilometers) instantly. The shock wave and high winds also destroy buildings and hurl objects through the air, crushing and stabbing human bodies. BLAST injuries could occur as far away as twelve to fifteen miles (twenty to twenty-four kilometers) from the center of a one-megaton explosion.

Burns. A nuclear explosion creates tremendous heat. A one-megaton nuclear explosion is hot enough to VAPORIZE anyone within a mile or more of GROUND ZERO. Human bodies within this range would be turned to gas and steam. Further from the explosion, the heat would cause severe second and third degree burns to almost everyone within ten miles (sixteen kilometers). The heat would also create a firestorm that would increase the number of burn injuries.

Radiation. A nuclear explosion creates huge amounts of radioactive material that may be spread by winds for hundreds of miles or more. Extremely high levels of RADIATION can cause death in hours. At lower levels, RADIATION SICKNESS may last for weeks or months before the victim either dies or recovers. Radiation can also cause cancer and birth defects many years after a person is exposed.

Disease. A nuclear explosion creates terrible problems of disease and infection. Clean water and proper waste disposal would not be available. Dead bodies would breed diseases. People with minor injuries would have trouble healing. Safe food would be in short supply. A nuclear explosion would also kill many doctors and nurses, and it would destroy the hospitals needed to treat the injuries caused by the explosion.

Medium-Range Ballistic Missile (MRBM)

A medium-range ballistic missile (MRBM) is a term sometimes used to describe an INTERMEDIATE RANGE BALLISTIC MISSILE that has a range from 700 miles (1,127 kilometers) to about 3,400 miles (5,474 kilometers). The PERSHING II is a U.S. medium-range missile, and its Soviet counterpart is the SS-20.

Megaton

A megaton is a unit used to measure the YIELD, or size of, a nuclear explosion. The prefix *mega* means "million." One megaton equals the explosive power of one million tons of TNT. The largest U.S. and Soviet nuclear WARHEADS ever DEPLOYED had the explosive power of about thirty megatons. The Soviets once tested a weapon of fifty-eight megatons, the world's largest nuclear explosion.

Most huge, multimegaton warheads are now obsolete (no longer useful). Instead, current MISSILES and bombers are designed to deliver many smaller weapons to their targets more accurately.

Midgetman

The Midgetman is the nickname for a proposed new U.S. INTERCONTINENTAL BALLISTIC MISSILE. It was suggested after military planners realized that large MISSILES with many WARHEADS make tempting targets for an enemy attack. The Midgetman would be a smaller missile that carries one warhead. To make the Midgetman a more difficult target for an enemy to destroy, it would be carried on a MOBILE LAUNCHER. The launchers would probably move from place to place over a large desert area.

Mike Shot

The Mike Shot was a U.S. NUCLEAR WEAPONS test that took place on Elugelab Island in the South Pacific Ocean on November 1, 1952. The Mike Shot was the first test of a full-scale FUSION (hydrogen) explosion. It was also the first nuclear explosion with a force greater than a million tons of TNT — about ten MEGATONS. The Mike device was not a deliverable nuclear weapon. However, its success led to the development of thermonuclear WARHEADS.

Millirem

A millirem is a unit that measures RADIATION exposure. It equals one-thousandth of a REM. An X RAY at the dentist's office exposes a person to about 10 millirems. The average person receives 170 millirems of radiation a year.

Mill Tailings

Mill tailings are the crushed rock that is a waste product of URANIUM mining. Since uranium ore is not very concentrated, large amounts of rock must be mined to obtain small amounts of the metal. The mill tailings left over after the ore is processed contain no uranium. But they still contain small amounts of other radioactive elements. Unlike other RADIOACTIVE WASTES, mill tailings are not stored carefully. Instead, they are left in huge piles at the mines. The RADIOACTIVITY from the tailings may get into water supplies or pollute the air. People exposed to such RADIATION might then be more likely to develop cancer.

Milstar Satellite

Milstar is a U.S. military communications satellite that will be put into orbit in the late 1980s. Using this satellite, U.S. military forces will be able to communicate with each other around the world. It is designed to transmit messages among U.S. forces during a nuclear war.

Minuteman II, Minuteman III Missiles

The Minuteman is the main U.S. INTERCONTINENTAL BALLISTIC MISSILE now in place. Both the Minuteman II and III are SOLID FUEL rockets that can be launched with a moment's notice. The Minutemen are based in underground silos in the states of Missouri, Nebraska, Wyoming, Montana, and North and South Dakota. The Minuteman II was first DEPLOYED in 1965. It carries a single one- or two-MEGATON WARHEAD and has a range of about 6,000 miles (9,660 kilometers). The United States has 450 of these MISSILES. The Minuteman III, deployed in 1970, carries

105

three warheads with YIELDS of 170 to 355 KILO-TONS each. The Minuteman III has a range of about 7,000 miles (11,270 kilometers). The United States has 550 Minuteman III missiles.

MIRV (see MULTIPLE INDEPENDENTLY TARGETABLE REENTRY VEHICLE)

Missile

A missile is a weapon that can be fired or launched toward a distant target. Modern missiles are powered by rocket engines. They are guided to their targets by computers, RADAR, and other electronic equipment.

Missile Gap

In 1960, presidential candidate John F. Kennedy claimed the Soviet Union was ahead of the United States in the ability to build INTERCONTINENTAL BALLISTIC MISSILES. Kennedy said this "missile gap" gave the Soviets a military advantage and left the United States open to attack.

Talking about the missile gap helped Kennedy win the U.S. presidential election. Later, military experts found there was no missile gap. U.S. missile technology was equal to or better than Soviet technology in the early 1960s.

Since that time, other politicians have talked about a "gap" between U.S. and Soviet technology. In the 1980 presidential election, candidate Ronald Reagan claimed the United States had a "WINDOW OF VULNERABIL-ITY." He said the Soviets had a big advantage in land-based MISSILES. This claim of a missile gap may have helped Reagan win that election, too.

Missile Silo

A missile silo is a huge concrete and steel structure built into the ground. It houses a MISSILE, which is fueled, armed, and ready to launch, as well as the equipment needed to launch the missile. All U.S. land-based ICBMs (MINUTEMAN II AND III, the MX) and many Soviet missiles are kept in silos. Missile silos are "HARD TARGETS," designed to resist any BLAST except a direct hit by a nuclear WARHEAD. Each silo is covered with a heavy door, which slides back to launch the missile inside.

The Air Force officers who control the missile are housed in an underground shelter miles away. Their commands are sent to the silo and its missile electronically. In the United States, the officers in one shelter control a squadron of ten missiles in ten different silos.

A U.S. intercontinental ballistic missile stands ready for launch in its underground missile silo.

Mobile Launcher

A mobile launcher is a trucklike vehicle that can carry a MISSILE from place to place. It also serves as a launching PLATFORM for the missile. Missiles on mobile launchers make a more difficult target for the enemy to hit than those on FIXED LAUNCHERS. The LANCE, PERSHING I AND II, and GROUND-LAUNCHED CRUISE MISSILES, are missiles designed for mobile launchers. The Soviet Union also has missiles, including the SS-20, that are carried on mobile launchers.

Moratorium

A moratorium is a temporary halt to an action or program such as the ARMS RACE. For example, in 1963 U.S. President John Kennedy declared a moratorium on NUCLEAR WEAPONS testing. At that time the United States stopped all NUCLEAR TESTS, and Kennedy invited the Soviet Union to do the same. The Soviets also temporarily halted their nuclear testing. Within two months the countries reached an agreement known as the PARTIAL TEST BAN TREATY.

On August 6, 1985, Soviet General Secretary Gorbachev declared a moratorium on all Soviet nuclear testing. He invited the United States to join that testing halt, and to discuss a TREATY ending all nuclear tests. The Reagan administration decided not to join the moratorium, and the United States kept on testing nuclear weapons. In February 1987, the Soviets ended their moratorium and began testing again.

Multilateral

Multilateral means having many sides. A multilateral TREATY is one that three or more countries sign. The NUCLEAR NON-PROLIFERATION TREATY is an example of a multilateral agreement. It has been signed by more than one hundred nations.

Multiple Independently Targetable Reentry Vehicle (MIRV)

A multiple independently targetable reentry vehicle (MIRV) is one of several nuclear WARHEADS carried on a single MISSILE. For example, each MINUTEMAN III MISSILE carries three MIRVs. One missile launches all three warheads, but during flight the warheads are sent toward separate targets.

The Minuteman III, DEPLOYED by the United States in 1970, was the world's first MIRVed missile. Soviet missiles began carrying MIRVed warheads in 1975. The latest U.S. and Soviet missiles carry even more MIRVed warheads. The MX missile can carry as many as ten warheads, and the new TRIDENT missile carries as many as fourteen MIRVs.

MIRVed missiles make ARMS CONTROL TREATIES harder to verify (check). Spy satellites can count missiles, but they cannot tell how many warheads each missile is carrying. To do that, an arms control inspector would have to take apart the missile.

Mururoa Atoll

Mururoa Atoll is an island in the South Pacific Ocean where France carries out all its NUCLEAR TESTS.

Mushroom Cloud

A mushroom cloud is the cloud of dust and smoke created by a nuclear BLAST. Extremely large non-nuclear explosions also create mushroom-shaped clouds. The mushroom cloud from a one-MEGATON nuclear explosion may be ten miles (sixteen kilometers) wide and fifteen miles (twenty-four kilometers) high.

A mushroom cloud carries thousands of tons of smoke, dust, and debris into the atmosphere. Much of this material is radioactive. As it settles back to earth, it spreads dangerous radioactive FALLOUT for hundreds of miles.

On July 16, 1945, the Trinity nuclear test produced this mushroom cloud in the New Mexico desert.

Mutually Assured Destruction (MAD)

Mutually Assured Destruction (MAD) means that in a nuclear war, the United States and the Soviet Union can be certain (assured) that both countries will be completely destroyed. Each country has enough NUCLEAR

WEAPONS to destroy the other, no matter which nation attacks first.

In theory, mutually assured destruction prevents war, because neither country would be foolish enough to attack the other. Mutually assured destruction has been a fact of nuclear STRATEGY since the mid-1960s. Since that time there has been no war between U.S. and Soviet forces. However, the strategy of mutually assured destruction must always work perfectly. One mistake could result in the destruction of both the United States and the Soviet Union.

MX

MX, which stands for "missile experimental," is the newest U.S. land-based INTERCONTINENTAL BALLISTIC MISSILE. President Reagan has named this MISSILE the "PEACEKEEPER," but most people still call it the MX. The first MX missiles were placed in their silos in late 1986.

Each MX carries ten independently targetable WARHEADS (MIRVs). Each warhead can be aimed with great ACCURACY. At least fifty of these new missiles will be built in the next several years.

Deciding whether or not to build the MX created much disagreement in the United States. Congress debated whether or not to spend billions of dollars to design and build the missile, and military experts couldn't agree on how to base it. Many different methods were suggested. These included MOBILE LAUNCHERS, new silos, or even carrying the missiles on trains or airplanes. The Reagan administration finally placed the MX in already existing silos, at least temporarily.

Another question was whether the new missile actually makes the United States safer. The MX is a COUNTERFORCE weapon, and MX warheads are accurate enough to destroy enemy missiles in hardened silos. The Soviet Union considers the MX a FIRST STRIKE weapon. During a crisis, the Soviets might decide to launch their missiles first, to keep them from being destroyed in their silos by the MX (see USE IT OR LOSE IT). For this reason, opponents of the MX think that it makes war more likely in a crisis. The U.S. government believes that the power and accuracy of the MX gives the United States a stronger nuclear DETERRENT (threat). As a result, it says, the new missile makes war less likely.

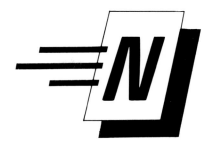

Nagasaki

Nagasaki is a city in southwestern Japan that was destroyed by a U.S. NUCLEAR BOMB on August 9, 1945. The bomb that was dropped on Nagasaki was the second nuclear bomb dropped on a Japanese city. The first U.S. bomb destroyed the city of HIROSHIMA three days earlier. Several days after Nagasaki was destroyed, Japan surrendered, ending World War II.

Nagasaki has been rebuilt. Today it is a busy port with a population of about one-half million people.

National Emergency Airborne Command Post (NEACP)

The National Emergency Airborne Command Post (NEACP) is a U.S. flying command center in a specially designed 747 jet. NEACP (pronounced *kneecap*) is also known by the code name Looking Glass. The United States has six NEACP planes. With refueling, these planes can stay airborne for several days.

NEACP can be used by the president or high-ranking military officials to direct a war from the air. It has modern communications equipment and computers. Flying in NEACP, U.S. leaders can receive information and send orders to military bases around the world.

National Military Command Center (NMCC)

The National Military Command Center (NMCC) is a command post located at the PENTAGON in Washington, D.C. It is "hardened" with steel and concrete to protect it from enemy attack. High ranking military leaders would use this command post in time of war or the danger of war. The United States has another military command center at a secret location. It also has a flying command post (see NATIONAL EMERGENCY AIRBORNE COMMAND POST).

National Technical Means

National technical means are methods that can be used to VERIFY (check) ARMS CONTROL TREATIES. These methods can be used without the cooperation of other countries. National technical means include spy satellites, long-range RADARS, radio listening posts, and seismic monitoring stations (to listen for underground explosions).

The other way to verify arms control treaties is through COOPERATIVE MEASURES. These methods can be used only with the cooperation of other countries.

NATO

North Atlantic Treaty Organization. NATO is a military alliance, a cooperative defense group that includes western European countries, the United States, and Canada. The European members of NATO are Great Britain, West Germany, France, Italy, Belgium, Denmark, the Netherlands, Norway, Portugal, Spain, Greece, Turkey, Iceland, and Luxembourg.

When this alliance was formed in 1949, the NATO nations agreed by TREATY to settle disputes among themselves peacefully. They also agreed to defend one another against military attacks from other countries. The military forces of the NATO countries plan STRATEGY together. They often hold military exercises and WAR GAMES to train and prepare their soldiers for war.

The United States has placed its NUCLEAR WEAPONS in several other NATO countries, including West Germany, the Netherlands, Italy, and Great Britain. Both Britain and France also have their own nuclear forces. In ARMS CONTROL talks, U.S. officials have insisted on discussing U.S. nuclear weapons separately from those of Britain and France. The Soviets have disagreed, saying that all NATO weapons should be considered together.

NAVSTAR

NAVSTAR is a system of U.S. satellites that makes it possible for ships, planes, and other U.S. forces to pinpoint their exact locations. Information provided by NAVSTAR satellites helps ships navigate, or chart, their courses. Among other things, the NAVSTAR system helps MISSILE submarines aim their long-range missiles much more accurately. NAVSTAR can also send navigation signals to BALLISTIC MISSILES in flight.

115

Negotiations

Negotiations are formal talks between people or countries that serve to settle disagreements peacefully. A TREATY may be the final result of negotiations between countries. In successful negotiations, both sides are satisfied with the final results.

Neutron

The neutron is one of the tiny particles that make up all ATOMS. Every atom is made of a NUCLEUS, surrounded by ELECTRONS. The nucleus of every atom (except hydrogen) contains both PROTONS and neutrons. Electrons are negatively charged, and protons are positively charged. Neutrons have no electric charge — meaning they are "neutral" — which is how they got their name.

Nuclear FISSION is caused by neutrons hitting the NUCLEI of URANIUM or PLUTONIUM atoms. When uranium or plutonium atoms split apart in nuclear explosions and NUCLEAR REACTORS, more neutrons are released as RADIATION. Neutrons are also given off in the FUSION reaction of THERMONUCLEAR (hydrogen) WEAPONS. Neutron radiation is extremely powerful and damaging to the human body.

Neutron Bomb

The neutron bomb is a NUCLEAR WEAPON that gives off large amounts of RADIATION with less explosive BLAST than other WARHEADS. It is also known as an "enhanced radiation weapon."

Neutron bombs are designed to kill people, while doing less damage to buildings than other nuclear warheads. In the 1970s, the U.S. government planned to place neutron warheads in Europe. Many people and groups protested against this idea, and President Carter decided against it.

The Reagan administration changed this policy. Neutron warheads are now part of the U.S. nuclear arsenal. Military plans call for them to be used as a weapon against large Soviet tank attacks.

Nevada Test Site

The Nevada Test Site is a large area of desert land 100 miles (161 kilometers) northeast of Las Vegas where the United States tests all its nuclear WARHEADS. The DEPARTMENT OF ENERGY carries out U.S. tests at the Nevada site. Great Britain also tests warheads in Nevada.

When the warheads explode deep underground, sensitive scientific instruments measure the effects of each BLAST. Outside the test site, the only noticeable effects are shock waves, similar to an earthquake. These can sometimes be felt hundreds of miles away.

During most tests, no RADIATION from the explosions escapes into the surrounding environment. But now and then some radioactive material leaks into the air from the underground explosions. The long-term effects of these leaks are hard to measure. The U.S. government says they are harmless.

No First Use

No first use is a government's promise never to be the first to use NUCLEAR WEAPONS in a war. A country with a no-first-use policy says it would use nuclear weapons only if an enemy uses them first.

Currently, the Soviet Union says it has a no-first-use policy. The United States does not. If Soviet forces attack western Europe with non-nuclear weapons, and if NATO forces are losing, the United States says it would use nuclear weapons.

Many people who are active in peace groups want the U.S. government to promise it will never again be the first to use nuclear weapons in a war. They believe such a promise would make relations between the United States and the Soviet Union less dangerous. The U.S. government believes the threat of nuclear weapons is needed to defend western Europe from a Soviet attack.

Non-Proliferation Treaty (see NUCLEAR NON-PROLIFERATION TREATY)

These antinuclear protestors in New York City gathered to express their opinions about nuclear weapons.

No Nukes

"No nukes" is a slogan sometimes used by U.S. antinuclear protestors to mean "no NUCLEAR WEAPONS." It can also mean "no nuclear power."

NORAD

North American Air Defense Command. NORAD is the headquarters for U.S. defense against an air or MISSILE attack. Located in CHEYENNE MOUNTAIN, Colorado, NORAD receives information from U.S. warning systems, including satellites and RADAR systems. This information is studied and analyzed with the aid of powerful computers. NORAD commanders then decide how U.S. forces should respond, and send out their orders. NORAD also commands all the jet fighters assigned to intercept enemy planes in an attack on U.S. territory.

Nuclear Accidents Agreement (see UNITED STATES-SOVIET UNION NUCLEAR ACCIDENTS AGREEMENT)

Nuclear Bomb

A nuclear bomb is a type of NUCLEAR WEAPON dropped from an aircraft. Since it has no power to propel itself, it must be dropped directly over its target by STRATEGIC BOMBERS or specially designed aircraft. Currently the United States has five types of nuclear bombs and is developing a sixth. The earliest nuclear weapons were atomic bombs such as the bombs dropped on HIROSHIMA and NAGASAKI.

Nuclear Depth Charge

A nuclear depth charge is a NUCLEAR WEAPON designed to destroy submarines. It can be dropped into the water from an airplane, or launched by rocket from a ship or attack submarine. Under water, the weapon explodes near an enemy submarine, destroying it (see ANTISUBMARINE ROCKET, SUBROC).

Nuclear Device

A nuclear device is another name for a nuclear explosive.

Nuclear Energy

Nuclear energy is the force that holds the NUCLEI of ATOMS together. Every atom is made up of negatively charged particles called ELECTRONS which surround a NUCLEUS. The nucleus is made of two different particles: positively charged PROTONS and neutral particles called NEUTRONS.

The nuclei of some substances, such as hydrogen, helium, carbon, and oxygen, are made up of relatively few particles. Others, such as lead, gold, URANIUM, and PLUTONIUM, have more than two hundred particles. It takes a great deal of nuclear energy to hold the particles in an atomic nucleus together. This energy is sometimes called "binding energy."

Under special conditions (see FISSION and FUSION), nuclear energy can be released. When this energy is released slowly, it can be used to make electricity in a NUCLEAR REACTOR. When it is released suddenly, the result is a nuclear explosion.

Nuclear Freeze

The Nuclear Freeze is a DISARMAMENT pro-posal. It suggests that both the United States and the Soviet Union stop testing, produc-ing, and deploying NUCLEAR WEAPONS. After a "freeze" on all new weapons, the two coun-tries would then talk about ways to lower the number of weapons they already have. Peo-ple who favor this plan think it would be a first step toward ending the ARMS RACE.

The Nuclear Freeze was first suggested in 1980. At that time the U.S. and Soviet nu-clear arsenals were about equal in strength. Since 1980, both countries have continued to build more nuclear weapons. However, most experts agree that the two countries are still about equal in nuclear arms.

In the early 1980s, the idea of a freeze became very popular. Opinion polls showed that more than 70 percent of the American people approved the idea. It gained support in many local and state elections, and the U.S. House of Representatives voted in favor of it.

People who favor a freeze say it would stop the arms race by preventing either side from building new and more dangerous weapons.

People who oppose a freeze say the United States needs to build new weapons in order to stay strong. They say it is this strength that prevents war.

Nuclear Free Zone

A nuclear free zone is an area where nuclear activities are restricted by law. The kinds of restrictions vary from place to place. Nuclear free zones may also be set up by TREA-TIES between countries.

For example, the TREATY OF TLATELOLCO makes all of Latin America a nuclear free zone. Through other treaties, the continent of Antarctica, many Pacific islands, the sea floor, and outer space have also been made nuclear free zones. In 1985, New Zealand declared its territory a nuclear free zone. U.S. warships with NUCLEAR WEAPONS were no longer allowed to dock there. In 1986, Iceland made a similar decision.

Many U.S. cities and towns have voted to become nuclear free zones. These local laws have little effect on U.S. government policy, but they do give people a way of expressing their opinions about the ARMS RACE.

Nuclear Non-Proliferation Treaty (NPT)

The 1968 Nuclear Non-proliferation Treaty (NPT) is an AGREEMENT among most of the world's nations. The TREATY is designed to limit the spread (proliferation) of NUCLEAR WEAPONS.

The signing nations that already had nuclear weapons — the United States, the Soviet Union, and Great Britain — promised not to give nuclear weapons material or technology to other countries. Other countries that did not have nuclear weapons promised not to build them. All the nations agreed to share the peaceful benefits of NUCLEAR ENERGY. The treaty also gave the INTERNATIONAL ATOMIC ENERGY AGENCY the job of checking on nuclear activities around the world.

The Nuclear Non-proliferation Treaty is still in effect. However, two nations with nuclear weapons, France and China, have not signed it. Several other countries which have, or will soon have, the ability to make nuclear weapons have also not signed. Those countries include India, Israel, Pakistan, South Africa, Brazil, and Argentina.

Nuclear Proliferation

Nuclear proliferation refers to the spread of NUCLEAR WEAPONS to countries that do not have them already. In 1945, only the United States had nuclear weapons, but since then, other countries have built them. The Soviet Union tested its first NUCLEAR BOMB in 1949. Great Britain, France, and China also have nuclear arms.

As more nations become technically advanced, many of them will be able to build nuclear weapons. The more countries that have nuclear weapons, the more likely it is that they will be used again. However, most countries have decided not to build nuclear weapons, even if they could.

Several countries other than those mentioned above have built nuclear weapons, or have the ability to do so. India has tested one nuclear bomb. Most experts agree that Israel has several hundred nuclear weapons. South Africa may also have tested a nuclear weapon. Still, none of these countries now says it possesses nuclear weapons.

Yet another group of nations probably does not have nuclear weapons today, but may be able to build them in the next few years. This group includes Pakistan, Brazil,

NUCLEAR NATIONS OF THE WORLD

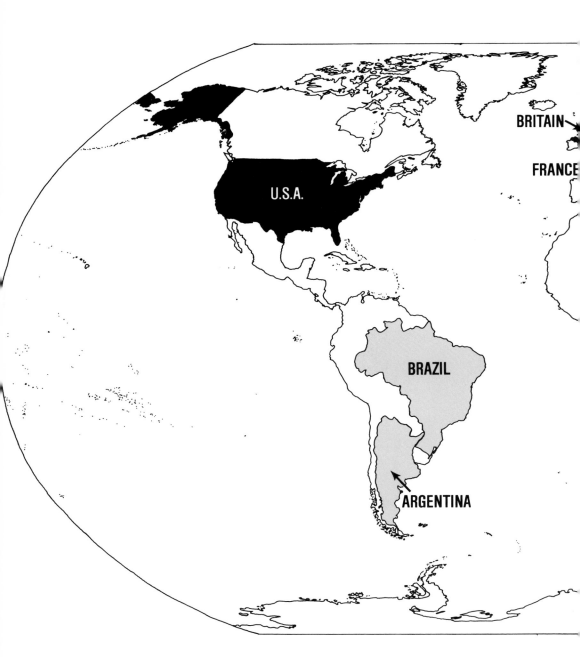

BRITAIN

FRANCE

U.S.A.

BRAZIL

ARGENTINA

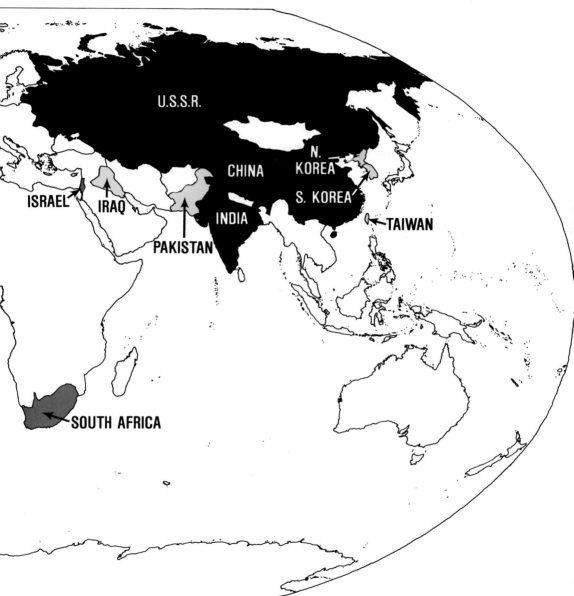

POSSIBLE "NEAR-NUCLEAR" COUNTRIES

PROBABLE NUCLEAR POWERS

NUCLEAR POWERS

U.S.S.R.

CHINA

N. KOREA

S. KOREA

ISRAEL

IRAQ

PAKISTAN

INDIA

TAIWAN

SOUTH AFRICA

Argentina, Iraq, Taiwan, North Korea, and South Korea. In the future, even more countries may be able to build nuclear weapons.

Nuclear Reactor

A nuclear reactor is a complex system of machinery that makes electrical power from the heat of nuclear FISSION. About sixty countries have at least one nuclear reactor. There are about nine hundred power reactors operating around the world.

Some nuclear reactors are specially designed to produce PLUTONIUM and TRITIUM fuel for NUCLEAR WEAPONS. These are called "PRODUCTION REACTORS." Nuclear reactors also provide power for many naval ships and submarines.

Most nuclear reactors are fueled by enriched URANIUM. As they make electricity, some of the reactor fuel changes into plutonium. As a result, any nation that has a reactor also has a possible source of fuel — plutonium — for nuclear weapons.

Nuclear Testing

Nuclear testing refers to experimental explosions of NUCLEAR WEAPONS, which are carried out for several purposes. Some tests are designed to discover how well new weapons designs work. Other tests study the effects of nuclear explosions on military equipment. These are known as "weapons effects tests." Finally, a few tests are done to determine if older weapons designs are still reliable.

Since the PARTIAL TEST BAN TREATY of 1963, all nuclear tests must be carried out underground. The United States tests all its nuclear weapons in the Nevada desert at the NEVADA TEST SITE. The main Soviet test site is at SEMIPALATINSK. French tests take place on MURUROA ATOLL in the South Pacific Ocean, and Chinese tests occur at LOP NOR.

Nuclear Waste (see RADIOACTIVE WASTE)

Nuclear Weapon

A nuclear weapon is the most powerful explosive known. In addition to its explosive power, a nuclear weapon also produces large amounts of harmful RADIATION. Some of this RADIOACTIVITY can last for years or even centuries.

The power of some nuclear weapons comes from splitting URANIUM or PLUTONIUM ATOMS (see FISSION WARHEAD). Most modern nuclear weapons produce their energy from the FUSION (joining) of hydrogen atoms (see THERMONUCLEAR WEAPON).

Not all nuclear weapons are bombs. MISSILES, CRUISE MISSILES, torpedos, artillery shells, and even hand-carried explosives can be armed with nuclear WARHEADS.

Nuclear Winter

Some scientists believe a nuclear war would produce a drastic cooling of the earth's climate. According to this theory, the dust and smoke from nuclear explosions and fires would block out much of the earth's sunlight. Without the sun's heat and light, the earth would become cold and dark. For several months there would be a nuclear winter. Exploding just a few hundred of the world's thousands of NUCLEAR WEAPONS might be enough to cause such a disaster.

A nuclear winter would kill much of the earth's plant and animal life. Plants need sunlight and warmth to grow. Animals need plants for food; without food, they, too, would die. Since human beings depend on plants and animals for food, they would also starve and die in a frozen world.

There is no way to test whether a nuclear winter would actually occur after a nuclear war. Predictions of a nuclear winter are based on studies of volcanic eruptions and huge fires. These events also throw smoke and dust into the atmosphere, although in much smaller amounts. From studying such events, scientists have found that a nuclear war would probably be followed by a nuclear winter. For this and many other reasons, a nuclear war can have no winners.

Nucleus, Nuclei

The nucleus is the center of an ATOM. Atomic nuclei are made up of two different types of particles, PROTONS and NEUTRONS. Protons have a positive electrical charge, while neutrons have no charge. The NUCLEAR ENERGY that holds an atomic nucleus together powers NUCLEAR REACTORS and NUCLEAR WEAPONS.

Nuke

Nuke is a slang word for a NUCLEAR WEAPON, or a NUCLEAR REACTOR. It is also used as a verb. "Nuke 'em" is a crude way of saying "Drop a nuclear weapon on them."

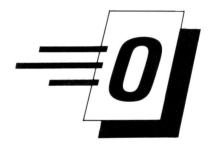

Oak Ridge, Tennessee

Oak Ridge is the location of a large U.S. NUCLEAR WEAPONS factory run by the Martin Marietta company. Most of the URANIUM for the bomb dropped on HIROSHIMA in 1945 came from Oak Ridge. The Oak Ridge plant makes all the uranium and LITHIUM DEUTERIDE fuel for the U.S. thermonuclear WARHEADS. A large nuclear waste dump is also located at Oak Ridge.

Oppenheimer, J. Robert (1904-1967)

J. Robert Oppenheimer was the scientist who led the MANHATTAN PROJECT, the U.S. research program that built the first NUCLEAR BOMBS during World War II. Oppenheimer was known for his ability to organize ideas. His leadership skills helped build the teamwork the Manhattan project needed to succeed.

After World War II, Oppenheimer spoke out against building thermonuclear (hydrogen) bombs. In 1954 he was accused of being a "security risk" because he had opposed the hydrogen bomb and had favored some ideas supported by communist groups in his younger years. From that time on, Oppenheimer was not allowed to do nuclear research. Oppenheimer believed NUCLEAR WEAPONS should be controlled by an international organization, such as the United Nations. He spent his last years as director of the Institute for Advanced Study at Princeton University.

In May 1944, Robert Oppenheimer *(left)* and Major W. A. Stevens went on a trip to select a site for the Trinity atomic bomb test.

Outer Space Treaty

The Outer Space Treaty is an AGREEMENT signed in 1967 by nearly one hundred countries, including the United States and the Soviet Union. Signers of the TREATY promised never to put NUCLEAR WEAPONS on the moon or in orbit around the earth.

The STRATEGIC DEFENSE INITIATIVE ("Star Wars") plan of the Reagan administration may include placing X-RAY LASERS in orbit around the earth. X-ray lasers are powered by nuclear explosives. If the United States carried out this part of the Strategic Defense Initiative plan, it would break the Outer Space Treaty.

Overkill

Overkill is extra firepower beyond what is needed to destroy an enemy. For example, the United States and the Soviet Union each have enough nuclear WARHEADS to destroy one another ten to twelve times or more.

In a single war, a nation can only be destroyed once. Military planners use overkill to guard against the failure of some of their weapons. For example, some MISSILES may fail to launch. Others may go off course, and still others may not explode. Overkill attempts to make sure that even if some weapons fail, the enemy will be totally destroyed.

Over-Pressure

Overpressure means pressure beyond or "over" normal air pressure. It is a measurement of the strength of the BLAST wave from an explosion. Overpressure is usually measured in pounds per square inch (see BLAST).

Ozone Depletion

One effect of a nuclear explosion is to deplete (reduce) the amount of ozone in the earth's upper atmosphere. Ozone is an oxygen molecule that has special properties. While ordinary oxygen has two oxygen ATOMS linked together, ozone has three. Surrounding the earth, the upper atmosphere has a layer that is rich in ozone. For life on earth, ozone's importance lies in its ability to absorb ultraviolet light.

Ultraviolet light is one part of sunlight. Most ultraviolet light is absorbed by the atmosphere's ozone layer before it can reach the earth's surface. That is important, because in large amounts ultraviolet light is dangerous to human beings. In small amounts ultraviolet light causes sunburn, and in large amounts it can cause severe burns and even blindness. Large amounts of ultraviolet light also make plants grow poorly.

Nuclear explosions send gases high into the atmosphere. Since some of these chemicals destroy ozone, a large number of nuclear explosions would destroy much of the earth's ozone layer. That would allow too much ultraviolet light to reach the earth's surface. Plants would be harmed, and animals and humans would be burned and blinded.

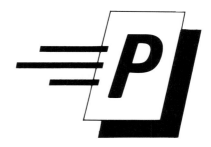

Pantex

The Pantex plant in Amarillo, Texas, is the factory that puts together all U.S. nuclear WARHEADS. Workers at this plant also take apart older warheads and use the parts from them to make new ones. From the Pantex factory, nuclear warheads are shipped by train or truck to military bases around the United States.

PARCS

Perimeter Acquisition Radar Attack Characterization System. PARCS is a U.S. RADAR station in North Dakota that is designed to track incoming Soviet MISSILE WARHEADS. Computers in the PARCS system can also predict where such warheads will strike.

Parity

Parity means equality. This term is usually used to describe military forces of equal strengths. U.S. and Soviet nuclear forces are now said to be in "ROUGH PARITY," meaning they are roughly equal in strength.

Partial Test Ban Treaty

The Partial (or Limited) Test Ban Treaty is an AGREEMENT that limits the types of nuclear WARHEADS tests that countries may conduct. It was signed in 1963 by the United States, the Soviet Union, and many other countries. Its official name is the "Treaty Banning Nuclear Weapons Tests in the Atmosphere, in Outer Space, and Underwater."

The TREATY does not allow any NUCLEAR WEAPONS tests in the atmosphere, in the ocean, and in space. However, it does allow underground warhead tests. Since it was signed more than twenty years ago, neither the United States nor the Soviet Union has broken the agreement.

In the 1940s, 1950s, and early 1960s, the United States and the Soviet Union tested their nuclear weapons above ground. U.S. and Soviet tests produced large amounts of radioactive FALLOUT that was carried around the globe. It was found in rain, in vegetables, and even in milk. People around the world were worried that the RADIOACTIVITY would cause cancer, especially among children. Countries that did not have nuclear weapons wanted to stop the fallout from U.S. and Soviet tests that was spreading across their lands.

The Partial Test Ban Treaty was signed partly because many people protested against NUCLEAR TESTING. The U.S. and Soviet governments also knew undergound tests would still allow them to test new weapons. The Partial Test Ban Treaty is one of the few success stories in the history of nuclear ARMS CONTROL.

Particle Beam Weapon

A particle beam weapon is a device, similar to a LASER, that would shoot a stream of high-energy atomic particles, such as ELECTRONS or PROTONS. Scientists working on the STRATEGIC DEFENSE INITIATIVE ("Star Wars") think particle beams might be used to destroy incoming enemy WARHEADS before they explode. Particle beam weapons have not yet been made to work successfully.

PAVE PAWS

Precision Acquisition of Vehicle Entry, Phased Array Warning System. PAVE PAWS is the U.S. RADAR system that warns against MISSILE attacks from submarines off the U.S. coast. It also can predict the targets of incoming WARHEADS.

Payload

Payload is the WARHEAD or other material that a MISSILE can launch into orbit, or at a target.

Peaceful Nuclear Explosions Treaty (PNE)

The Peaceful Nuclear Explosions Treaty (PNE) is a 1976 AGREEMENT between the United States and the Soviet Union. It sets rules for underground nuclear explosions that are used for peaceful purposes such as mining or digging canals.

Peacekeeper

Peacekeeper is the U.S. government name for the newest U.S. INTERCONTINENTAL BALLISTIC MISSILE. It is more commonly known as the MX.

Peace Through Strength

"Peace through strength" refers to the current U.S. policy for dealing with rival countries such as the Soviet Union. According to this idea, the United States will remain at peace as long as it has strong military forces. If it maintains its strength, no other country will dare to take advantage of the United States by attacking it.

President Reagan is a strong supporter of the peace through strength policy. During his two terms in office, the Reagan administration greatly increased the amount of money the U.S. government spends on weapons and military equipment. Most members of the U.S. Congress and many American citizens also believe in the idea of peace through strength.

Penetrating Bomber

A penetrating bomber is an airplane designed to carry bombs through enemy air defenses. Modern penetrating bombers must be fast and agile. They must be able to avoid RADAR detection, and they must have methods of avoiding antiaircraft MISSILES.

Pentagon

The Pentagon is the huge headquarters building for the U.S. DEPARTMENT OF DEFENSE. It is located in Arlington, Virginia, across the Potomac River from Washington, D.C. The Pentagon is an unusual building because it has five sides.

Permissive Action Link (PAL)

A permissive action link (PAL) is an electronic lock attached to many U.S. NUCLEAR WEAPONS. It is designed to prevent accidental nuclear launches and explosions. A code must be entered into the PAL before a WARHEAD can be armed and fired. If someone enters the wrong code, the warhead will not explode.

Not all U.S. nuclear warheads have PALs. U.S. SUBMARINE-LAUNCHED BALLISTIC MISSILES use another system instead (see FAIL DEADLY). Some U.S. tactical nuclear weapons do not have PALs either.

Pershing I, Pershing II Missiles

The Pershing I and II are U.S. nuclear MISSILES. Both missiles are carried on trucklike MOBILE LAUNCHERS and carry single nuclear WARHEADS. They are DEPLOYED (placed) in western Europe.

The Pershing I has a range of 460 miles (740 kilometers) and is considered a short-range or TACTICAL NUCLEAR WEAPON. The Pershing II has a range of about 1,100 miles (1,771 kilometers) and is considered an INTERMEDIATE-RANGE BALLISTIC MISSILE.

Because of its range, the Pershing II has caused concern in Europe. From its German bases, it can reach targets in the western Soviet Union in just six to ten minutes. As a result, Soviet defense officials have very little time to decide if they are being attacked, or if their RADARS are giving them a false signal. Because of this short warning time, some Europeans and Americans are afraid that the Pershing IIs make an accidental nuclear war more likely.

Pine Tree Line

The Pine Tree Line refers to a series of RADAR stations across southern Canada that are designed to track Soviet bombers approaching the United States from the north. The Pine Tree radar stations were built during the 1950s. They are operated by both the United States and Canada.

Platform

Platform is a military term for any vehicle from which nuclear MISSILES can be launched. For example, a TRIDENT submarine is a platform for launching Trident missiles. A B-52 bomber can be a platform for launching CRUISE MISSILES or SHORT-RANGE ATTACK MISSILES.

Plutonium

Plutonium is a heavy, radioactive metal. One ISOTOPE (variety) of plutonium, Pu-239, is used as the fuel for NUCLEAR WEAPONS or reactors. It takes only about ten pounds (less than five kilograms) of plutonium to make a NUCLEAR BOMB. Another isotope, Pu-238, is used to power heart pacemakers. Plutonium is not found naturally on earth. Pu-239 is made from URANIUM 238 in NUCLEAR REACTORS and is also produced as a waste product in nuclear power plants.

Plutonium is extremely active chemically. Because it burns when exposed to oxygen, it must be kept away from air at all times. It has a radioactive HALF-LIFE of 24,100 years meaning that it will lose half of its RADIOACTIVITY over that period of time. Plutonium is also one of the most deadly substances known.

A microscopic speck of it can cause lung cancer in a person.

Polaris

The Polaris was the first U.S. SUBMARINE-LAUNCHED BALLISTIC MISSILE. The first Polaris submarine was launched in 1960. Since then all U.S. Polaris MISSILES have been replaced with POSEIDON and TRIDENT missiles. However, Great Britain still has four submarines that carry Polaris missiles. They have a range of 2,500 miles (4,025 kilometers), and each missile can carry as many as six nuclear WARHEADS.

Polar Route

The shortest path between the United States and Europe and Asia crosses the arctic (north polar) regions. MISSILES launched to and from the United States and the Soviet Union would follow such a path, called the polar route. Because of that route, most U.S. missile and RADAR stations are located in the northern part of the country and in Canada.

Poseidon

The Poseidon is the second U.S. SUBMARINE-LAUNCHED BALLISTIC MISSILE. First placed on submarines in 1971, the Poseidon is much more accurate than the POLARIS, and carries a larger payload. It has a range of 2,500 to 2,800 miles (4,025 to 4,508 kilometers).

Each Poseidon MISSILE carries as many as fourteen WARHEADS, and each Poseidon submarine carries sixteen missiles. The United States has thirty-one Poseidon submarines.

However, twelve of these ships now carry the newer, even more accurate TRIDENT missiles.

Post-Boost Vehicle (see BUS)

Preemptive Attack

A preemptive attack is a FIRST STRIKE with NUCLEAR WEAPONS. In a preemptive attack, one country uses its weapons against the weapons of another country. Its goal is to prevent the other country from using its weapons against the country making the preemptive attack.

Production

Production refers to the actual building of NUCLEAR WEAPONS. A nuclear weapon goes through DEVELOPMENT and testing before it can be produced and DEPLOYED.

Production Reactor

A production reactor is a specially designed NUCLEAR REACTOR that makes PLUTONIUM and TRITIUM fuel for NUCLEAR WEAPONS. U.S. production reactors are located at the SAVANNAH RIVER PLANT in South Carolina and the HANFORD RESERVATION in Washington state.

Proliferation (see NUCLEAR PROLIFERATION)

Protocol

A protocol is a signed AGREEMENT between two or more nations. A protocol is often an addition to, or a change in, a TREATY.

For example, the ABM TREATY of 1972 allowed both the Soviet Union and the United

States to build two ANTIBALLISTIC MISSILE sites. Later, in 1974, the two countries signed a protocol that reduced this number to one site apiece.

Proton

The proton is one of the tiny particles that make up all ATOMS. Every atom is made of a NUCLEUS, surrounded by ELECTRONS. The nucleus of every atom (except hydrogen) contains both protons and NEUTRONS. Electrons are negatively charged, and protons are positively charged. Neutrons have no electric charge — meaning they are "neutral" — which is how they got their name.

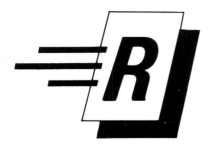

RAD

Radiation Absorbed Dose. The rad is a unit that measures the amount of IONIZING RADIATION absorbed by any living or non-living material. A dose of one rad equals about one ROENTGEN or about one hundred dental X RAYS. Nuclear workers are allowed to absorb no more than five rads per year. Human exposure to RADIATION is usually measured in REMS rather than rads.

Radar

Radio detection and ranging. Radar is a method of finding objects (detection) at long distances using radio waves. Radar also can tell how far away these objects are (ranging), and even determine their size and shape.

A radar antenna sends out radio signals. The signals bounce off objects such as airplanes or ships and reflect back to the antenna. By measuring the strength of the reflected signal, and how long it takes to return, a radar system can determine the size and distance of an object.

Radar is an essential part of a defense against an attack by airplanes and MISSILES. Radar is also used by attacking aircraft and missiles to help them find their targets.

Radiation

Radiation is energy emitted (given off) by substances. Every object in the universe emits some radiation, most often in the form of heat. Light is also a type of radiation. Other more powerful forms of radiation, called IONIZING RADIATION, are emitted by radioactive substances (see ALPHA RADIATION, BETA RADIATION, GAMMA RADIATION, IONIZING RADIATION, NEUTRON, THERMAL RADIATION, and X RAY).

Radiation Sickness

Radiation sickness is the disease caused by exposure to IONIZING RADIATION. RADIATION damage is much more severe if the whole body is exposed, instead of only a small part of the body. Also, some kinds of cells are more sensitive to radiation than others.

Any whole-body dose greater than 50 to 75 REMS causes radiation sickness and 600 rems or more is usually deadly to humans. Extremely large doses of radiation (1,000 rems or more) destroy the nervous system, killing a person in several hours, or even minutes. No treatment is possible. Radiation of 600 rems or more destroys the lining of the intestines, causing vomiting, internal bleeding, and dehydration. The victim dies within several days. Again, no treatment is possible.

Lower doses of radiation (75 to 500 rems) damage the body's bone marrow. Without bone marrow, a person cannot make new blood cells. If the bone marrow is destroyed, this form of radiation sickness is usually fatal. However, bone marrow transplants from healthy people can save some victims. If the marrow is only damaged, the victim will suffer from weakness, bleeding, and infection. These symptoms may last for weeks or months before the person eventually dies or recovers.

People who are exposed to low levels of radiation may develop health problems many years later. They may have an increased chance of developing cancer or having children with birth defects. However, these long-term problems are not considered "radiation sickness."

The day after an atomic bomb destroyed much of Nagasaki, Japan, a dazed woman and child search for food. Many people who survived the explosion later became ill with or died from radiation sickness.

Radioactive Decay

Radioactive decay is the process by which radioactive ATOMS give off RADIATION. Each time they emit radiation, they become a different type of atom.

For example, an atom of the radioactive element PLUTONIUM 239 decays by giving off a beta particle. It becomes URANIUM 235. The U-235 then emits another beta particle and decays into thorium 231. This process continues until the atom changes into a stable (non-radioactive) type of atom. An atom of plutonium eventually becomes an atom of non-radioactive lead.

Radioactive Waste

Radioactive wastes are the waste products left over from activities that use radioactive substances. Nuclear power plants and NUCLEAR WEAPONS manufacturing produce thousands of tons of radioactive wastes each year. URANIUM mining and medical and industrial uses of radioactive substances also produce radioactive wastes.

Radioactive wastes are divided into five categories: HIGH-LEVEL WASTE, LOW-LEVEL WASTE, SPENT FUEL, TRANS-URANIC WASTE, and MILL TAILINGS. Since all of them release RADIATION, they all pose some danger to humans and animals. However, some forms of radioactive wastes are much more dangerous than others.

Because certain forms of radioactive wastes remain dangerous for thousands of years, disposing of them is a big problem. Such wastes must be buried in a place where they will never be disturbed. Right now the United States has only temporary storage sites for its high-level wastes and spent (used) nuclear fuel. (see HIGH-LEVEL NUCLEAR WASTE, LOW-LEVEL NUCLEAR WASTE, MILL TAILINGS, SPENT FUEL, and TRANS-URANIC WASTE).

Radioactivity

Radioactivity is the property, or quality, of certain materials that emit (give off) RADIATION. Some substances found on earth, such as URANIUM, radium, and thorium, are naturally radioactive. Other substances become radioactive in a NUCLEAR REACTOR or nuclear explosion. Some of these artificially radioactive materials stay radioactive for only a short time. Others may remain radioactive for hundreds or thousands of years.

Radioactive substances emit several forms of radiation (see ALPHA RADIATION, BETA RADIATION, GAMMA RADIATION, NEUTRON, and X RAY).

Rail Gun

A rail gun is a weapon that shoots non-explosive projectiles at very high speeds. It is a type of KINETIC ENERGY WEAPON — a weapon that destroys targets by colliding with them. Rail guns fire their "bullets" by propelling them along a pair of rails, using electrical or magnetic force. Experimental rail guns have been built and tested, but no working rail gun weapons yet exist.

Rail guns may become a part of the Reagan administration's STRATEGIC DEFENSE INITIATIVE ("Star Wars"). Like the recently tested antisatellite missiles, they would be used to shoot down incoming enemy WARHEADS.

Ratification

Ratification means approval. All TREATIES that the U.S. government makes with other countries must be ratified, or agreed to, by the U.S. Senate. The executive branch of the U.S. government (the president and his advisors) makes a treaty, but the treaty doesn't go into effect until the Senate ratifies it. Two-thirds of the Senate must vote in favor of a treaty to ratify it.

Reactor (see NUCLEAR REACTOR)

Reentry Vehicle

A reentry vehicle is the heat-resistant casing that covers the WARHEAD of a BALLISTIC MISSILE. During its flight, a ballistic missile rises above the atmosphere. When an object falls back into the atmosphere from space, the air rubbing against it creates extremely high temperatures. The reentry vehicle protects the warhead from this heat, allowing it to reach its target.

Relay Mirror

A relay mirror is one proposed part of the Reagan administration's STRATEGIC DEFENSE INITIATIVE ("Star Wars"). Positioned in orbit high above the earth, a relay mirror would reflect LASER beams from their energy sources on earth to orbiting satellites. The satellites would then focus the beams on enemy MISSILES, destroying them. Relay mirrors and the laser weapons they would work with do not yet exist.

REM

Roentgen Equivalent, Man. The rem is a unit that measures the amount of RADIATION to which a human being has been exposed. Some forms of radiation are more harmful than others. Rem measurement takes that difference into account. One rem is the amount of any kind of radiation that equals the damage done by one ROENTGEN of X RAYS.

The average U.S. citizen is exposed to about 170 millirems each year (1 millirem equals 1/1000 rem). An X ray at the dentist amounts to around 10 millirems. Any dose of more than 50 to 75 rems will result in some RADIATION SICKNESS. A dose of 600 rems or more is almost always fatal to humans.

Reprocessing

Reprocessing is a complicated series of chemical steps that recycles the used fuel rods of NUCLEAR REACTORS. Part of the reprocessed fuel rods can be reused as reactor fuel. Highly radioactive PLUTONIUM is one of the waste products in SPENT FUEL. Reprocessing removes the plutonium from those fuel rods. The plutonium may then be used to fuel nuclear reactors or to make NUCLEAR WEAPONS.

U.S. power companies do not reprocess fuel. Instead, they just store it. However, other countries around the world do reprocess their nuclear fuel. As a result, the world's supply of plutonium is constantly growing. Keeping this plutonium safe is becoming a greater concern.

Retaliation

Retaliation means striking back. Countries with NUCLEAR WEAPONS threaten to retaliate with those weapons if they are attacked by another nation. That means they will use their nuclear weapons to strike back at the country that attacks them.

Rocky Flats, Colorado

Rocky Flats, near Denver, Colorado, is the location of a large U.S. NUCLEAR WEAPONS factory. At the Rocky Flats plant, PLUTONIUM metal is formed into the correct shape and size for nuclear WARHEADS. These bomb parts are then sent to the PANTEX plant in Texas to be built into warheads. In past years, several serious accidents at Rocky Flats have leaked plutonium into the environment.

Roentgen

The roentgen is the unit scientists use to measure how much X RADIATION or GAMMA RADIATION is absorbed by a substance. It is named in honor of Wilhelm Roentgen, the scientist who discovered X RAYS. One roentgen is a large amount of radiation. An X ray at the dentist's office is only about one-hundredth of a roentgen.

Rongelap

Rongelap is an island in the Pacific Ocean. In 1954, FALLOUT from the BRAVO U.S. NUCLEAR TEST polluted the island. The test itself took place on BIKINI ATOLL, more than 100 miles (161 kilometers) away. The people living on Rongelap got RADIATION SICKNESS and were forced to leave their island. The same nuclear test poisoned a Japanese fishing boat, killing one crew member and injuring twenty-two others.

Rough Parity

Rough parity is a phrase which describes two different military forces that are about equal in strength. Most experts believe the United States and the Soviet Union now have rough parity in nuclear forces.

The nuclear forces of the two countries are not exactly equal. The Soviet Union has more land-based MISSILES, while the United States has more submarine-based missiles. Also, the Soviet Union has more MEGATONS of explosive power, but the United States has a larger number of WARHEADS. Nevertheless, the total nuclear forces of the two countries are roughly equal in strength.

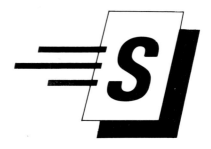

SAC (see STRATEGIC AIR COMMAND)

SALT I, SALT II (see STRATEGIC ARMS LIMITATION TREATY)

Sandia National Laboratory

Sandia National Laboratory in Albuquerque, New Mexico, is one of three research laboratories where new U.S. NUCLEAR WEAPONS are designed. The laboratory is run for the U.S. government by the AT&T company. Researchers at Sandia specialize in designing and testing non-nuclear parts of U.S. nuclear weapons.

Satchel Charge

A satchel charge is an explosive that can be carried by a person. It is also known as a "suitcase bomb." U.S. weapons designers have created a NUCLEAR BOMB small enough to fit in a suitcase. It could be carried into a city and hidden, to be exploded later by a timer or a radio signal.

Satellite Early Warning System (SEWS)

The Satellite Early Warning System (SEWS) is a set of three U.S. satellites in orbits high above the earth. They are at just the right altitude so that they stay directly above the same spot on the earth's surface at all times. Such a special orbit is called a "geosynchronous orbit."

These satellites watch the earth's surface for signs of MISSILE launches. They are designed to give the United States an early warning of an enemy missile attack.

Savannah River Plant

The Savannah River plant, in South Carolina near the Georgia border, is a U.S. NUCLEAR WEAPONS factory. Run by the Dupont company for the U.S. government, it produces all the PLUTONIUM, DEUTERIUM, and TRITIUM fuel for U.S. nuclear weapons. The plant has five NUCLEAR REACTORS for producing plutonium and tritium. It has factories that separate the plutonium and tritium from other reactor products and a factory that separates HEAVY WATER (containing deuterium) from ordinary water. The Savannah River plant also has a large storage dump for RADIOACTIVE WASTE. Much of this waste is HIGH-LEVEL NUCLEAR WASTE that comes from making plutonium.

SDI (see STRATEGIC DEFENSE INITIATIVE)

Sea-Bed Treaty

The Sea-bed Treaty, which was signed in 1971, outlaws NUCLEAR WEAPONS on or under the sea floor. This TREATY has been signed by all nations with nuclear weapons, except

France. More than eighty other countries have also signed the treaty.

Semipalatinsk

Semipalatinsk is the site where the Soviet Union tests most of its NUCLEAR WEAPONS. This major Soviet test site is located in eastern Kazakhstan, in the south central part of the Soviet Union.

Shock Wave (see BLAST)

Short-Range Attack Missile (SRAM)

A short-range attack missile (SRAM) is a guided MISSILE carried by U.S. bombers. The SRAM has a range of about 100 miles (161 kilometers) and carries a single nuclear WARHEAD. U.S. bombers carry these missiles in place of bombs so that the planes can attack their targets from many miles away. Attacking from a distance makes it less likely that the bombers will be shot down before they destroy their targets.

Short-Range Ballistic Missile (SRBM)

A short-range ballistic missile (SRBM) is a MISSILE that can carry a WARHEAD to a target less than 700 miles (1,127 kilometers) away. It is called a BALLISTIC MISSILE because its warhead follows an arching path. Because of their short range, these weapons are considered tactical, rather than strategic, nuclear weapons. U.S. short-range ballistic missiles include the LANCE and PERSHING I. Soviet SRBMs are the SS-21, SS-22, and SS-23 (see SS-MISSILE).

Shroud

A shroud is the outer covering on the nose of a BALLISTIC MISSILE. It protects WARHEADS while they are boosted above the atmosphere. Once the MISSILE is outside the atmosphere, the shroud opens to uncover and release the warheads and the post-boost vehicle (BUS) that carries them.

Silo (see MISSILE SILO)

Single Integrated Operations Plan (SIOP)

The Single Integrated Operations Plan (SIOP) is the overall U.S. plan for fighting a nuclear war. The purpose of SIOP, whose details are kept secret, is to prepare the nation's armed forces for a nuclear war. SIOP includes targets and STRATEGIES for many possible wartime situations.

Soft Target

A soft target is a target that has not been "hardened" to resist a nuclear BLAST. Cities, factories, power plants, and transportation centers are examples of soft targets (see HARD TARGET).

Solid Fuel

Solid fuel is the type of fuel used in most modern MISSILES. INTERCONTINENTAL BALLISTIC MISSILES were once fueled with liquid fuels, which are highly explosive and hard to handle. Solid fuels can be stored safely in missiles for long periods of time. Because they are already loaded with fuel, solid fuel missiles are ready to be launched at a moment's notice.

Space-Based Defenses

Space-based defenses are a part of the Reagan administration's suggested STRATEGIC DEFENSE INITIATIVE ("Star Wars"). Space-based defenses could include LASERS, PARTICLE BEAM WEAPONS, and RAIL GUNS. Placed in satellites orbiting the earth, these weapons would be designed to shoot down enemy missiles (see STRATEGIC DEFENSE INITIATIVE).

Space Mine

A space mine is an ANTISATELLITE WEAPON. Space mines would take the form of small, explosive satellites. They could be placed in orbit beside military communications satellites, or satellites that are part of the proposed "Star Wars" space-based defense. In case of war, space mines could be exploded, destroying nearby military satellites.

Spent Fuel

Spent fuel is a dangerous type of nuclear waste—the used fuel rods from NUCLEAR REACTORS. It is highly radioactive and produces a great deal of heat. It also contains dangerous radioactive elements.

Spent fuel can be reprocessed, or separated, into different elements. Some of it can then be reused to produce more electricity. One product of REPROCESSING is PLUTONIUM, which can also be used to make nuclear WARHEADS. Some countries with nuclear power plants reprocess their spent fuel. The United States does not. Instead, spent fuel from U.S. reactors is kept in temporary storage. Sooner or later, the U.S. government must decide how to get rid of this nuclear waste product.

Splitting the Atom (see FISSION)

SS-Missile

SS followed by a number refers to the U.S. method (NATO code) for naming Soviet land-based MISSILES. Each of these missiles carries one or more nuclear WARHEADS, and most carry several warheads. The SS-17, -18, -19, -24, and -25 are the Soviets' current INTERCONTINENTAL BALLISTIC MISSILES. The SS-20 is an INTERMEDIATE-RANGE BALLISTIC MISSILE, and the SS-21, -22, and -23 are SHORT-RANGE BALLISTIC MISSILES.

SS-N-Missile

SS-N followed by a number refers to the U.S. method (NATO code) for naming Soviet SUBMARINE-LAUNCHED BALLISTIC MISSILES. These MISSILES all carry one or more nuclear WARHEADS. Many carry several warheads.

Stability

Stable means steady or balanced. In the vocabulary of the ARMS RACE, "stability" is a situation that is not likely to lead to war. For example, if two countries have equal levels of military force, neither country has an advantage over the other. That is considered a stable situation.

Stand-Off Weapon

A stand-off weapon is a NUCLEAR WEAPON that can be fired at a target from a ship or a plane many miles away. Using stand-off weapons allows the plane or ship to fire its weapons before it comes under enemy attack. A SHORT-RANGE ATTACK MISSILE is an example of a stand-off weapon. A SRAM can be launched from a bomber when it is as far as 100 miles (161 kilometers) from its target. This makes it unnecessary for the plane to fly directly over its target to drop bombs.

START (see STRATEGIC ARMS REDUCTION TALKS)

Star Wars (see STRATEGIC DEFENSE INITIATIVE)

Stealth Bomber, Stealth Fighter

The stealth bomber is a new long-range bomber that the United States plans to design and build. It is called "stealth" because the materials the plane will be made of, and its shape, will make it hard to detect by RADAR. Stealth bombers will also fly at high speeds and low altitudes to avoid being located by radar. Designs for this new airplane are secret, but experts suggest it may look like some kind of "flying wing."

The stealth fighter has already been built. Known as the F-19, this plane is also hard to detect by radar. The stealth fighter is one of the U.S. Air Force's most closely guarded secrets.

157

Strategic Air Command (SAC)

The Strategic Air Command (SAC) is the branch of the U.S. Air Force that operates long-range bombers (B-52S and B-1BS). It also operates long-range land-based nuclear MISSILES such as the MINUTEMAN MISSILE and MX. SAC's headquarters are located in an underground command post in Omaha, Nebraska.

Strategic Arms Limitation Treaty (SALT I and II)

The Strategic Arms Limitation treaties (SALT I and II) resulted from a series of talks between the United States and the Soviet Union. The goal of the talks was to control the number and types of NUCLEAR WEAPONS each nation could have. The SALT talks were suggested by President Lyndon Johnson in 1967. They began in 1969, while Richard Nixon was the U.S. president and Leonid Brezhnev was the leader of the Soviet Union.

The SALT I TREATIES were completed in 1972. They had two main parts. One part limited the number of land-based and submarine-launched nuclear MISSILES DEPLOYED by each country. This part of the AGREEMENTS is usually called the SALT I Treaty. That treaty also allowed each nation to modernize its missiles, and to use multiple WARHEADS (MIRVs). As a result, the nuclear ARMS RACE continued even after the treaty was signed. The other part of the SALT I agreements, which limits the ANTIBALLISTIC MISSILE SYSTEMS of each country, is usually called the ABM TREATY.

The SALT II talks continued the process that had begun with SALT I. The SALT II

Treaty was signed by President Carter and Soviet General Secretary Brezhnev in 1979. This treaty limited each country to 2,250 long-range nuclear launchers (missiles and bombers). It also limited the total number of strategic warheads each nation can have, and allowed both countries to develop one new INTERCONTINENTAL BALLISTIC MISSILE.

Some members of the U.S. Congress believed the treaty gave the Soviets a military advantage. Many U.S. citizens were also angry because the Soviets had just sent soldiers into Afghanistan. As a result, the U.S. Senate refused to ratify (approve) the treaty. Nevertheless, the U.S. and Soviet governments agreed to follow the treaty limits.

In 1981, President Reagan decided not to work towards a SALT III treaty. Instead, he proposed a new set of ARMS CONTROL talks, called the STRATEGIC ARMS REDUCTION TALKS. Meanwhile, both the U.S. and Soviet governments followed the limits set by SALT II.

In 1986, President Reagan announced that the United States would no longer follow the SALT II limits. The Soviet Union replied that if the United States went beyond the SALT II limits, it would, too. In late 1986, the U.S. government broke the limits it had agreed to observe in SALT II.

Strategic Arms Reduction Talks (START)

The Strategic Arms Reduction Talks (START) are ARMS CONTROL talks between the United States and the Soviet Union. President Reagan began these talks in 1982, after he ended the SALT talks. According to the Reagan administration, the purpose of START is to reduce the numbers of U.S. and Soviet long-range NUCLEAR WEAPONS. Through late 1987, no agreement had yet been reached on controlling strategic, or long-range, missiles.

Strategic Bombers

Strategic bombers are long-range airplanes that can carry large loads of NUCLEAR WEAPONS from one continent to another. The United States now has two strategic bombers, the B-52 and the B-1B. Most U.S. bombers carry CRUISE MISSILES or SHORT-RANGE ATTACK MISSILES rather than bombs. The Soviet Union also has many strategic bombers. The U.S. military calls current Soviet bombers the BEAR, BADGER, BLINDER, BACKFIRE, and BLACKJACK.

Strategic Defense Initiative (SDI)

The Strategic Defense Initiative (SDI) is the Reagan administration plan for defending against attacking INTERCONTINENTAL BALLISTIC MISSILES. It is also known as "Star Wars." According to the plan, SDI would work in several stages.

The defense would begin when an enemy launched its MISSILES. SDI satellites orbiting the earth would fire beams of LASER light or atomic particles (such as NEUTRONS or PRO-

TONS) at the missiles. These beams would destroy some of the missiles during their BOOST PHASE, which lasts about five minutes (see X-RAY LASER).

A second stage of the SDI defense would destroy more WARHEADS as they coast above the atmosphere on their way to their targets. For this stage, the weapons used would be satellite-based lasers, particle beams, or RAIL GUNS. Rail guns shoot heavy non-explosive bullets at extremely high speeds.

The third stage of the SDI defense would destroy some of the remaining warheads as they reenter the atmosphere and fall toward their targets. Small, high-speed missiles, ground-based beam weapons, and rail guns would fire on approaching warheads.

SDI has more critics than any other program now planned by the U.S. military. Many scientists doubt it will work. Even its supporters say it will not stop all the missiles from a Soviet attack. In fact, some warheads would make it past all the defenses and explode at their targets. People who oppose SDI say even if the weapons work as planned, they could be defeated. For example, an enemy could use DECOY warheads to fool the defenses. It could also fire low-flying missiles and CRUISE MISSILES that satellites could not destroy.

Some critics of SDI believe it could make nuclear war more likely. Suppose one country had an antimissile defense like SDI. That country might be more likely to launch an attack, because it might think it could survive a return attack from the small number of missiles that its enemy would have left.

Because of this possibility, the enemy might feel forced to attack before the missile defense was put in place.

Despite all the arguments against it, SDI is a popular idea. Many people think that if the United States has a way to protect the nation from a nuclear attack, it should use that defense.

Strategic Weapons

Strategic weapons are long-range NUCLEAR WEAPONS. They are able to reach an enemy's territory from their point of launch. INTERCONTINENTAL BALLISTIC MISSILES, SUBMARINE-LAUNCHED BALLISTIC MISSILES, and long-range bombers are all considered strategic weapons.

The United States and the Soviet Union use strategic weapons for DETERRENCE. They threaten each other with them, to promote their own national interests around the world. In 1987, the United States had about 12,000 strategic WARHEADS. The Soviet Union had about 9,000 strategic warheads.

Strategy

Strategy means planning. It is the overall, long-range plan for military operations. Strategic planning takes events throughout the whole world into account. Strategy is used to give a country a military advantage before any fighting breaks out. In addition to military plans, modern national strategy includes political and economic planning as well. *Strategy* is usually distinguished from TACTICS, which means battlefield planning.

Strontium 90

Strontium 90 is an ISOTOPE (variety) of the element strontium. It has a radioactive HALF-LIFE of about twenty-eight years. Strontium 90 is produced in nuclear explosions, and later falls to earth as FALLOUT.

In the 1950s, strontium 90 from U.S. and Soviet NUCLEAR TESTS was discovered in milk. Scientists also found traces of it in children's baby teeth. Many people were afraid the radioactive strontium could cause bone cancer in children. This worry caused many people to call for a nuclear test ban. Public concern about strontium 90 in milk played a large part in convincing the U.S. and the Soviet governments to sign the PARTIAL TEST BAN TREATY of 1963.

Submarine-Launched Ballistic Missile (SLBM)

Long-range BALLISTIC MISSILES carried on submarines (SLBMs) form a large part of U.S. and Soviet nuclear forces. The British, French, and Chinese also have smaller numbers of SLBMs.

SLBMs are carried in launching tubes aboard submarines. The first submarine-launched ballistic missile was the POLARIS, which was DEPLOYED by the United States in 1960. All Polaris submarines are now retired from service. In 1971, the United States launched the first of thirty-one submarines that carry POSEIDON MISSILES. Each submarine carries sixteen missiles, and each Poseidon missile carries ten or fourteen WARHEADS. The newest U.S. missile-launching submarine carries TRIDENT missiles. First launched in 1981, each submarine carries twenty-four Trident missiles, and each missile carries as

163

many as ten warheads. Just one Trident submarine has enough firepower to destroy every major city in the Soviet Union. The United States plans to build a fleet of twelve to twenty Trident vessels. Soviet submarine-launched ballistic missiles are known by the letters SS-N followed by a number, such as the SS-N-6.

Modern missile-launching submarines are powered by NUCLEAR REACTORS instead of diesel engines. That means they can cruise quietly beneath the surface for weeks or months at a time, hidden in the vast oceans. Most nuclear missile submarines would survive the first stages of a nuclear war. They could then launch their missiles to strike back against the enemy.

SUBROC

A subroc is a short-range MISSILE carried on a U.S. submarine. It is a nuclear depth charge, a weapon designed to destroy an enemy's submarines. The Soviet Union also has similar weapons. A subroc is launched underwater from a torpedo tube. It travels to the surface, flies through the air for as far as thirty miles (forty-eight kilometers), and then dives back underwater to explode near its target.

Suitcase Bomb (see SATCHEL CHARGE)

Summit Meeting

A summit meeting is a meeting between the top leaders of two or more countries. In the past, U.S. and Soviet leaders have used summit meetings as occasions to discuss or sign important TREATIES and AGREEMENTS.

Super Bomb

"Super bomb" was an early nickname for THERMONUCLEAR (hydrogen) WEAPONS. The term "super bomb" was often used in the late 1940s and early 1950s.

Surface-to-Air Missile (SAM)

A surface-to-air missile (SAM) is a rocket-powered weapon fired either from the ground or from a surface ship towards a target in the air. SAMs can be used to destroy aircraft or incoming MISSILE WARHEADS.

Surface-to-air missiles are guided by computers and RADAR, or other electronic sensors. Most SAMs are armed with conventional high explosives. Some surface-to-air missiles can also be armed with nuclear warheads.

Surface-to-Surface Missile (SSM)

A surface-to-surface missile (SSM) is a rocket-powered weapon fired either from the ground or from a surface ship toward a target that also lies on the earth's surface. Surface-to-surface missiles are usually short-range tactical weapons, guided by computers and RADAR, or other electronic sensors. A surface-to-surface missile may be armed with a nuclear WARHEAD or with high explosives.

Szilard, Leo (1898-1964)

Leo Szilard was a Hungarian-born physicist who moved to the United States in the 1930s to escape the Nazis. Along with fellow scientist Eugene Wigner, he convinced ALBERT EINSTEIN to write his famous letter to President Franklin D. Roosevelt. Einstein's letter warned the president that German scientists were looking for ways to build a NUCLEAR BOMB. During World War II, Szilard worked on the MANHATTAN PROJECT. With ENRICO FERMI, he created the world's first nuclear CHAIN REACTION.

Szilard was concerned about the actual use of NUCLEAR WEAPONS. After Germany surrendered, he wrote a petition asking President Truman not to use the ATOMIC BOMB against Japan. Many of his fellow scientists on the Manhattan Project signed Szilard's petition.

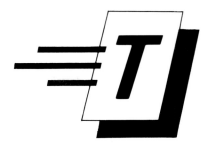

Tactical Nuclear Weapons

Tactical nuclear weapons are NUCLEAR WEAP-
ONS intended for use in battle. Tactical weapons are also known as "battlefield nuclear
weapons." Compared to STRATEGIC WEAPONS,
they usually have less explosive power. However, tactical nuclear weapons still are enormously destructive compared to CONVEN-
TIONAL (non-nuclear) WEAPONS. Many of them
are more powerful than the bomb that destroyed HIROSHIMA.

Tactical nuclear weapons come in many
forms, including bombs, short-range MIS-
SILES, torpedos, depth charges, artillery shells,
land mines, and underwater mines. The
United States has at least 15,000 tactical nuclear weapons, and the Soviet Union probably has at least 12,000 similar weapons.

U.S. tactical nuclear weapons are under
the control of military field commanders
(generals and admirals). U.S. forces in Europe have many such weapons, and they are
carried on many U.S. Navy ships.

Unlike strategic (long-range) weapons, tactical weapons are not kept under central control. Because they are stored at many places
around the world, some people worry that
they might be stolen by terrorists or used
accidentally.

167

Tactics

Tactics are methods used by military commanders to manage their forces on the battlefield. *Tactics* refers to the use of troops and weapons in battle. By comparison, STRATEGY refers to a much wider kind of planning that involves longer periods of time and larger areas of territory.

Teller, Edward (1908-   )

Edward Teller is the nuclear scientist who is most responsible for developing the thermonuclear (hydrogen) bomb. Born in Hungary, he came to the United States in 1935 to escape the Nazis. Teller worked on the MANHATTAN PROJECT, helping to build the first FISSION bombs. After World War II, he was the strongest voice in favor of building THERMONUCLEAR WEAPONS and became the chief designer of the first thermonuclear bomb.

Teller has been a long-time supporter of keeping the peace by staying militarily strong. He believes in a powerful U.S. nu-

Edward Teller is sometimes called "the father of the hydrogen bomb."

clear arsenal. In recent years, Teller has also supported the Reagan administration's STRATEGIC DEFENSE INITIATIVE ("Star Wars").

Teller-Ulam Configuration

The Teller-Ulam configuration is the basic design for THERMONUCLEAR (hydrogen) WEAPONS. It was created by EDWARD TELLER and Stanislaw Ulam. The design focuses the powerful RADIATION of a FISSION explosion inward on a supply of FUSION fuel (lithium hydride). The radiation sets off a thermonuclear reaction in the fusion fuel. Until recently, the Teller-Ulam configuration was one of the world's most closely kept secrets (see THERMONUCLEAR WEAPON).

Test Ban (see COMPREHENSIVE TEST BAN TREATY and PARTIAL TEST BAN TREATY)

Thermal Pulse

The thermal pulse is the tremendous burst of heat produced by a nuclear explosion. The effects of this heat vary, depending on the distance from the center of the explosion. In the explosion of a one-MEGATON WARHEAD, almost everything within a mile (1.6 kilometers) of GROUND ZERO would be VAPORIZED. It would be so hot that objects, animals, and people would be turned into gases, like the steam from a boiling teakettle.

Farther from the center of the explosion, the THERMAL RADIATION would cause severe burns and start vast fires (see FIRESTORM). The thermal effects of a one-megaton BLAST would extend for ten miles (sixteen kilometers) or more from the center of the explosion.

Thermal Radiation

Thermal radiation is heat. One of the first effects of a nuclear explosion is an enormous burst of heat (see THERMAL PULSE). Temperatures at the center of a nuclear BLAST reach millions of degrees.

Thermonuclear Weapon

A thermonuclear weapon is a FUSION weapon, often known as a "hydrogen bomb." It has much greater power than a FISSION weapon fueled with URANIUM or PLUTONIUM. A thermonuclear weapon produces its power as the NUCLEI of hydrogen ATOMS fuse (join) to form helium. As this happens, huge amounts of energy are released.

U.S. scientists created the first fusion explosion in 1951, and three years later they made the first fusion bomb small enough to be used as a weapon. The Soviets first tested a thermonuclear weapon in 1953. Most of the WARHEADS in the current U.S. and Soviet arsenals are thermonuclear weapons.

A fusion reaction can only happen under tremendous temperatures and pressures. In thermonuclear warheads, a fission explosion fueled with uranium or plutonium sets off the fusion explosion. In the warhead, LITHIUM DEUTERIDE (a compound of LITHIUM and DEUTERIUM) is the fuel for the fusion reaction. When the fission bomb explodes, its extremely high temperature and RADIATION are focused on the lithium deuteride. This heats and squeezes the fusion fuel, setting off the fusion reaction. The lithium absorbs NEUTRONS and changes into TRITIUM. The tritium and deuterium nuclei then fuse, to become helium nuclei. This fusion process releases tremendous amounts of energy.

In most modern warheads, the fusion fuel is surrounded by a layer of uranium 238. The high-energy neutron radiation from the fusion sets off a fission reaction in the U-238. This adds to the force of the explosion and creates large amounts of radioactive FALLOUT. All the events in a thermonuclear explosion happen in millionths of a second.

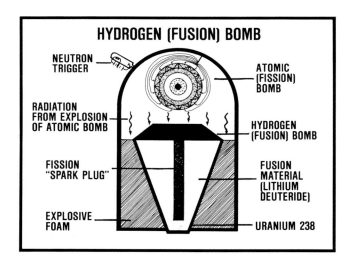

Throw Weight

Throw weight is the amount of weight that a MISSILE can carry toward its targets. The greater the throw weight of a missile, the larger the WARHEAD or the more warheads it can lift. In general, Soviet INTERCONTINENTAL BALLISTIC MISSILES have greater throw weights than U.S. missiles.

Advances in technology have made warheads much smaller, which, in turn, has made throw weight less important. A warhead from the new U.S. MX missile is just six feet (less than two meters) long. It weighs only about 500 pounds (227 kilograms). Yet this warhead has the explosive force of 300 KILOTONS, about twenty times the power of the HIROSHIMA bomb. Ten of these warheads are carried on each missile.

Titan II

The Titan II was a U.S. INTERCONTINENTAL BALLISTIC MISSILE which was based in underground silos in the Midwest. The last Titan IIs were taken out of service in 1986.

The Titan MISSILE was fueled with LIQUID FUEL and had a range of about 8,000 miles (12,880 kilometers). Each Titan missile carried one nine-MEGATON WARHEAD. Liquid fueled rockets can be dangerous. In 1980 a Titan missile exploded in its silo in Arkansas, killing one worker and injuring several others. The explosion also tossed the missile's warhead through the air over the length of two football fields. Fortunately, it did not explode.

Tomahawk

Tomahawk is the name of the U.S. CRUISE MISSILE. It can be launched from submarines, surface ships, ground-based MOBILE LAUNCHERS, or aircraft, and has a range of about 1,300 miles (2,100 kilometers). The Tomahawk is only about twenty feet (six meters) long and just two feet (less than a meter) in diameter. Its small size makes it easy to move and hide. It can carry either a nuclear WAR-HEAD or conventional high explosives. The Tomahawk has a very accurate computer guidance system, and is difficult to detect by RADAR because it flies so close to the ground.

Trans-Uranic Waste

Trans-uranic wastes are waste materials that contain radioactive elements heavier than URANIUM. Included in this group of materials are PLUTONIUM and other elements created in nuclear reactions. Most trans-uranic wastes are produced in NUCLEAR WEAPONS factories and nuclear power plants. In the United States, trans-uranic wastes are kept in temporary storage, usually at the locations where they are created. The U.S. government has not yet decided how to dispose of these wastes permanently.

Treaty

A treaty is a written AGREEMENT between two or more countries. Treaties are negotiated for the United States by the executive branch of the government (the president and his advisors). To take effect, a treaty must then be ratified, or approved, by the U.S. Senate.

Since the nuclear ARMS RACE began in 1945, there have been several treaties dealing with nuclear weapons. (For details on specific treaties, see ABM TREATY, ANTARCTIC TREATY, NUCLEAR NON-PROLIFERATION TREATY, OUTER SPACE TREATY, PARTIAL TEST BAN TREATY, PEACEFUL NUCLEAR EXPLOSIONS TREATY, SEA-BED TREATY, STRATEGIC ARMS LIMITATION TREATY, TREATY OF TLATELOLCO, and the UNITED STATES-SOVIET UNION NUCLEAR ACCIDENTS AGREEMENT.)

Treaty of Tlatelolco

The Treaty of Tlatelolco makes South America, Central America, and the Caribbean Sea area a NUCLEAR-WEAPONS-free zone. The TREATY was signed by twenty-five countries in 1967. As part of the agreement, all the nuclear powers promise not to bring nuclear weapons into Latin America. They also promise not to use nuclear weapons against any signers of the treaty. Cuba is the only Latin American country that has not signed the Treaty of Tlatelolco. However, the treaty is not yet in force in Brazil, Argentina, or Chile.

Triad

A triad is something made of three parts. In the vocabulary of the ARMS RACE, triad means the three parts of the U.S. and Soviet strategic nuclear arsenals. These are intercontinental bombers, land-based INTERCONTINENTAL BALLISTIC MISSILES, and SUBMARINE-LAUNCHED BALLISTIC MISSILES.

Trident, Trident II

The Trident MISSILES are the newest U.S. SUBMARINE-LAUNCHED BALLISTIC MISSILES. They are fired from submarines hidden below the surface of the ocean, and have a range of more than 2,500 miles (4,000 kilometers). The Trident I missile, also known as the C-4, carries as many as eight nuclear WARHEADS. The Trident II, known as the D-5, carries eight to fourteen nuclear warheads.

The newest version of the Trident is more accurate than other submarine-launched ballistic missiles. A Trident II warhead is designed to land within a few hundred yards of its target. Because it is so accurate, the Trident II could be considered a FIRST-STRIKE weapon. It can destroy enemy missiles in their silos before they can be launched.

Each new Trident submarine carries twenty-four D-5 missiles. The United States plans to build twelve to twenty Trident submarines, and by 1987, five had already been completed. Trident I missiles have also replaced older POSEIDON missiles on some Poseidon submarines.

Trinity Nuclear Test

Trinity was the name of the first test of a NUCLEAR WEAPON. The Trinity test took place in the desert near Alamogordo, New Mexico, on July 16, 1945. The bomb exploded in this test was built by the scientists of the MANHATTAN PROJECT. It was armed with PLUTONIUM. Rather than being dropped from a plane, it was exploded at the top of a steel tower.

Many of the scientists who had worked on the Trinity bomb watched the test from sev-

This picture shows the site in the New Mexico desert where Manhattan Project scientists prepared for the Trinity test explosion on July 16, 1945.

eral miles away. J. ROBERT OPPENHEIMER, director of the Manhattan Project, said he thought of a passage from Indian (Hindu) scriptures as he watched the explosion: "I have become Death, the destroyer of worlds."

Tritium

Tritium is an ISOTOPE (variety) of hydrogen. Ordinary hydrogen ATOMS have one PROTON and no NEUTRONS in their NUCLEUS. Tritium has one proton and two neutrons. Since the extra neutrons make the atom heavier, tritium is sometimes called "HEAVY HYDROGEN." It is one of the fuels used in a thermonuclear (hydrogen) bomb. Tritium is radioactive, and has a HALF-LIFE of twelve years. It is produced from the element LITHIUM in NUCLEAR REACTORS and in nuclear explosions.

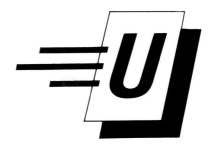

U-235 (see URANIUM)

U-238 (see URANIUM)

Unilateral

Unilateral means having one side. In the vocabulary of the nuclear ARMS RACE, unilateral means action taken by one country, even if other countries do not agree to take similar actions. For example, in 1963, the United States unilaterally stopped testing NUCLEAR WEAPONS above ground. President Kennedy invited the Soviets to do the same. Two months later, the two countries agreed on the PARTIAL TEST BAN TREATY. Another unilateral testing halt began in 1985. The Soviet Union stopped all its NUCLEAR TESTS and invited the United States to negotiate a TREATY banning all nuclear testing.

"Unilateral disarmament" would mean that one country would get rid of its nuclear weapons, whether other countries kept theirs or not. It is very unlikely that any country would decide to disarm unilaterally. That would leave it in a very weak military position.

United States-Soviet Union Nuclear Accidents Agreement

The United States-Soviet Union Nuclear Accidents Agreement was signed in 1971. According to its terms, each country promises to tell the other immediately if it has an accidental launch or an explosion of a NUCLEAR WEAPON. In such a time of crisis, leaders of the two nations use the HOTLINE to communicate.

Uranium

Uranium is a radioactive metal, and the heaviest chemical element that occurs naturally on earth. Uranium is found naturally in three different ISOTOPES, or varieties. U-238 is by far the most common — more than 99 percent of natural uranium is U-238. U-238 has 92 PROTONS and 146 NEUTRONS in its NUCLEUS. The radioactive HALF-LIFE of U-238 is about 4½ billion years. About .7 percent of natural uranium is U-235. U-235 has 92 protons and 143 neutrons. It has a half-life of about 700 million years. U-235 is the isotope that can produce the FISSION CHAIN REACTION needed for NUCLEAR REACTORS and NUCLEAR WEAPONS. A tiny fraction of natural uranium is U-234, the third isotope.

Before it can be used for reactors or weapons, uranium must be "enriched." That means the U-235 must be concentrated. For reactors, the uranium must be 3 to 5 percent U-235, and for nuclear weapons, the uranium must be 85 to 95 percent U-235. Enrichment is done by several complicated industrial processes (see ENRICHED URANIUM).

U-238 is also used in nuclear weapons and reactors. In THERMONUCLEAR (hydrogen) WEAPONS, U-238 may be wrapped around the FU-

SION WARHEAD. The fusion explosion causes the U-238 to undergo fission, which can double the power of the explosion. In nuclear reactors, U-238 is changed into PLUTONIUM. Because it is so heavy, U-238 is also used in non-nuclear armor-piercing shells.

Huge amounts of ore must be mined and processed to gather small amounts of uranium. Large deposits of uranium ore are found in the United States, Canada, South Africa, Niger, France, and Australia. In addition, the Soviet Union and China probably have large supplies of uranium. Information about their uranium supplies is kept secret. In the United States, uranium is mined in Colorado, Wyoming, Utah, New Mexico, and Texas.

Use It Or Lose It

"Use it or lose it" is a phrase that describes a strategic problem of the nuclear ARMS RACE. The problem is this: Both the United States and the Soviet Union have accurate MISSILES aimed at each other's missiles. During a crisis, each side may suspect the other is going to launch a nuclear FIRST STRIKE. If a country is attacked, many of its missiles will be destroyed before they can be fired. For this reason, each nation may be tempted to attack first, before the other one destroys its weapons. In other words, if a nation does not use its missiles first, it may lose them in an attack. This problem creates an unstable situation. Because of it, when the two countries have a serious disagreement, they will both be more likely to use their missiles, starting a nuclear war.

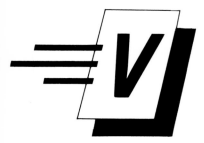

Vaporize

Vapor is gas or steam. Vaporize means evaporate—to turn from a solid into a gas. Temperatures in a nuclear explosion are so high that solid objects, including human beings, are vaporized, or turned into gas and steam.

Verification

Verify means to check, or prove something to be true. In the nuclear ARMS RACE, verification means checking to make sure that countries keep the promises they have made in arms control TREATIES. There are many ways to verify agreements between the United States and the Soviet Union, or between other countries. These methods are usually divided into "NATIONAL TECHNICAL MEANS" and "COOPERATIVE MEASURES."

Cooperative measures are methods in which countries must work with one another to verify their treaty. For example, each country could allow inspectors from the other country to observe its military activities. In another method, both sides could allow inspectors from a neutral country to do the checking.

National technical means are methods that can be used to verify a treaty even without the other country's cooperation. Both the United States and the Soviet Union have technology that allows them to discover what other countries are doing. For example, satellites with sensitive cameras can spot movements of equipment and materials, and watch the work at weapons factories. Radio "listening posts" can tune in to secret missile tests, and long-range RADARS can follow the paths of the MISSILES. Seismic recorders, like those used to measure earthquakes, can "hear" underground nuclear explosions.

To be a success, any arms control treaty must have verification methods built into it. Each side must be sure that the other side is living up to its part of the bargain. Otherwise, one side or the other may break the agreement. That would start a new stage of the arms race all over again.

VLF

Very Low Frequency. (see EXTREMELY LOW FREQUENCY)

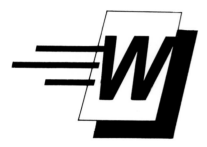

War Games

War games are practice sessions that train armies or military leaders for actual warfare. War games allow military leaders to try different STRATEGIES and TACTICS. They also test new weapons and equipment and give troops battlefield experience.

Some war games are played on computers, using computer programs that are written to create lifelike battle situations. In these games, military commanders give orders to the computers. The computers then calculate the results of the commanders' decisions.

Warhead

A warhead is the explosive part of a MISSILE, bomb, or other weapon. The word *warhead* may be used to describe nuclear or non-nuclear explosives. A modern nuclear warhead is quite small. An MX warhead, for example, is about six feet (less than two meters) long and weighs about 500 pounds (227 kilograms). This small object has the explosive power of 300,000 tons of TNT. A 170-KILOTON CRUISE MISSILE warhead is about the same size as a large trash can.

Warning Shot

Some military planners have suggested that when there is a serious threat of war, the United States might fire a nuclear "warning shot." This would be a single nuclear explosion. It would warn the enemy that if it did not back down, the United States would launch a larger nuclear attack. Such a warning shot might convince an enemy to end its threat. However, it also might lead the enemy to fight back with its own NUCLEAR WEAPONS.

Warsaw Pact

The Warsaw Pact is an AGREEMENT among the Soviet Union and neighboring Communist countries of eastern Europe. The nations of the Warsaw Pact include the Soviet Union, Poland, Hungary, East Germany, Czechoslovakia, Bulgaria, and Romania. This military alliance was formed in 1955, partly as a response to the creation of NATO. The Warsaw Pact countries have agreed to help defend one another in case of attack. Like NATO, the Warsaw Pact often holds war games to give the troops from the different countries practice working together.

Weapons-Grade Uranium

Weapons-grade uranium is URANIUM that contains enough U-235 to be used in nuclear WARHEADS. To reach that level, uranium must be enriched to at least 85 percent U-235. Uranium with lower amounts of U-235 can be used in nuclear power plants, but not in weapons. NUCLEAR REACTORS that power ships and submarines are also fueled with weapons-grade uranium.

Window of Vulnerability

In his 1980 presidential campaign, Ronald Reagan said the United States had a weakness in its nuclear forces. He called this weakness the "window of vulnerability," which meant that the Soviet Union had many more land-based MISSILES than the United States did. President Reagan said the Soviets would be able to destroy most U.S. missiles in their silos, leaving the United States without a way to strike back. After he was elected, President Reagan tried to correct this "weakness" by building the new MX missile.

Many experts thought President Reagan's "window of vulnerability" did not really exist. They believed the U.S. advantage in submarine-launched nuclear missiles made up for the Soviet advantage in land-based missiles. If that was the case, the armed forces of the two nations were in a situation of ROUGH PARITY, or about equal.

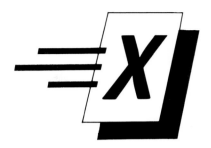

X Ray

X rays are a powerful form of RADIATION. First discovered by Wilhelm Roentgen in 1895, X rays are a form of electromagnetic radiation, like light or radio waves. X rays have no weight and no electrical charge. They travel at the speed of light (186,000 miles, or 300,000 kilometers per second). Since X rays are powerful enough to pass through living flesh, they are useful in examining broken bones and other medical problems. In a nuclear explosion, X rays are produced in huge amounts. Because they are so powerful, they can do great damage to human cells.

X-Ray Laser

The X-ray laser is one of the weapons in the proposed STRATEGIC DEFENSE INITIATIVE ("Star Wars"). Actual X-ray laser weapons do not yet exist. These "nuclear-pumped lasers" could be carried in satellites orbiting the earth. They could also be DEPLOYED on MISSILES, ready to be launched into space as soon as an enemy's missiles are launched. Each X-ray laser would contain a thermonuclear WAR-HEAD surrounded by many lenses.

A nuclear explosion produces huge amounts of X rays. The lenses of a laser satellite would focus these X rays at the rockets lifting the enemy warheads toward the United States. The lenses would be pointed at many rocket boosters all at once. When the warhead exploded, powerful bursts of X rays would burn holes in the attacking missiles, destroying them. A split second later, the laser satellites would be destroyed by the thermonuclear explosion.

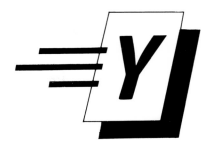

Yellowcake   Yellowcake is a URANIUM oxide compound which is produced after uranium ore is milled and purified. It is called yellowcake because of its bright yellow coloring.

Yield   Yield is the measurement of the explosive power of a nuclear WARHEAD. Yield is measured in KILOTONS or MEGATONS.

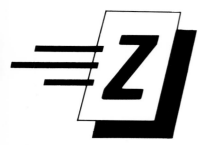

Zero Option

The zero option (sometimes called the zero-zero or DOUBLE ZERO OPTION) is an ARMS CONTROL proposal suggested by the Reagan administration in 1981. The zero option means that both the United States and the Soviet Union would remove all their intermediate-range NUCLEAR WEAPONS from Europe. The zero option might also include removing short-range nuclear MISSILES. In 1987 the two nations agreed in principle to accept this proposal as the basis for an arms control agreement.

Appendix

National Organizations Working to Bring the Nuclear Arms Race under Control

This list of organizations includes those that may be of particular interest to students, parents, and teachers. There are many others. For a complete list of organizations, see *The Peace Catalog* or *Peace Resource Book*, listed in the bibliography.

American Friends Service Committee, 1501 Cherry St., Philadelphia, PA 19102

Another Mother for Peace, 407 N. Maple Dr., Beverly Hills, CA 90210

Children's Campaign for Nuclear Disarmament, 14 Everit St., New Haven, CT 06511

Children's Creative Response to Conflict, Box 271, Nyack, NY 10960

Common Cause, 2030 M St., NW, Washington, D.C. 20036

Concerned Educators Allied for a Safe Environment, c/o Schirmer, 17 Gerry St., Cambridge, MA 02138

Council for a Livable World, 11 Beacon St., Boston, MA 02108

Educators for Social Responsibility, 23 Garden St., Cambridge, MA 02138

Fellowship of Reconciliation, P.O. Box 271, Nyack, NY 10960

Friends of the Earth, 1045 Sansome, #404, San Francisco, CA 94111

Greenpeace USA, 2007 R St., NW, Washington, D.C. 20009

Ground Zero, P.O. Box 19049, Portland, OR 97219

INFACT, 310 E. 38th St., Rm. 301, Minneapolis, MN 55409

International Association of Educators for World Peace, P.O. Box 3282, Huntsville, AL 35810

Jobs With Peace, 77 Summer St., Boston, MA 02110

League of Women Voters, 1730 M St. NW, Washington, D.C. 20036

Nuclear Free America, 325 E. 25th St., Baltimore, MD 21218

Nuclear Weapons Freeze Campaign, 220 I St. NE, Washington, D.C. 20002

Peace Links: Women Against Nuclear War, 747 8th St. SE, Washington, D.C. 20003

People United to Save Humanity (PUSH), 930 E. 50th St., Chicago, IL 60615

Physicians for Social Responsibility, 200 Third St. SE, Washington, D.C. 20003

SANE, 711 G St. NW, Washington, D.C. 20003

Union of Concerned Scientists, 26 Church St., Cambridge, MA 02238

United Campuses to Prevent Nuclear War, 1346 Connecticut Ave. NE, Washington, D.C. 20036

War Resisters League, 339 Lafayette St., New York, NY 10012

Women's Action for Nuclear Disarmament, New Town Station, Box 153, Boston, MA 02258

Women's International League for Peace and Freedom, 1213 Race St., Philadelphia, PA 19107

Women Strike for Peace, 145 S. 13th St., Philadelphia, PA 19107

Selected Bibliography

The books listed below have been selected for their value as resources and/or for their appropriateness for upper elementary, junior high, and high school age students. The reading levels of these books vary widely. Some, such as Dr. Seuss's *The Butter Battle Book*, are written with simple vocabularies, but are good for starting discussions. Others are written at adult reading levels, but provide excellent sources of information about the nuclear arms race.

Bender, David ed. *The Arms Race: Opposing Viewpoints*. St. Paul, Minnesota: Greenhaven Press, 1985.

———. *Nuclear War: Opposing Viewpoints*. St. Paul, Minnesota: Greenhaven Press, 1985.

Calder, Nigel. *Nuclear Nightmares: An Investigation into Possible Wars*. New York: Penguin, 1981.

Chant, Christopher, and Ian Hogg. *Nuclear War in the 1980s?* New York: Harper and Row, 1983.

Cloud, Kate, et. al. *Watermelons, Not War*. Philadelphia: New Society Publishers, 1984.

Coerr, Eleanor. *Sadako and the Thousand Paper Cranes*. New York: Dell, 1979.

Dennis, Jack, ed. *The Nuclear Almanac*. Redding, Massachusetts: Addison-Wesley, 1984.

Ford, Daniel, Henry Kendall, and Steven Nadis. *Beyond the Freeze*. Union of Concerned Scientists. Boston: Beacon Press, 1982.

Ground Zero. *Nuclear War: What's In It for You?* New York: Pocket Books, 1982.

Hersey, John. *Hiroshima*. New York: Knopf, 1946.

Institute for Defense and Disarmament Studies. *Peace Resource Book*. Cambridge, Massachusetts: Ballinger Publishing, 1986.

League of Women Voters Education Fund. *The Nuclear Waste Primer*. Nick Lyons Books, 1985.

Maruki, Toshi. *Hiroshima No Pika*. New York: Lothrop, Lee, and Shepard, 1980.

Moore, Melinda, and Laurie Olsen. *Our Future at Stake: A Teenager's Guide to Stopping the Nuclear Arms Race*. Washington, D.C.: Citizens Policy Center, 1984.

Schell, Jonathan, *The Fate of the Earth*. New York: Knopf, 1982.

Sedacca, Sandra. *Up in Arms*. Washington, D.C.: Common Cause, 1984.

Seuss, Dr. *The Butter Battle Book*. New York: Random House, 1984.

Sivard, Ruth Leger, *World Military and Social Expenditures* (annual), World Priorities, Box 25140, Washington, D.C., 20007.

Streiber, Whitley. *Wolf of Shadows*. New York: Knopf, 1985.

Sweeney, Duane, ed. *The Peace Catalog*. Seattle, Washington: Press for Peace, 1984.

Sweet, William. *The Nuclear Age*. Washington, D.C.: Congressional Quarterly, 1984.

Tsipis, Kosta. *Arsenal*. New York: Simon and Schuster, 1984.

U.S. Arms Control and Disarmament Agency, *Arms Control and Disarmament Agreements*, Washington, D.C.: 1980.